And
JESUS
will be born

Also by Adrian Plass

A Year at St Yorick's
Adrian Plass Classics
An Alien at St Wilfred's
Clearing Away the Rubbish
Colours of Survival (with Bridget Plass)
From Growing Up Pains to the Sacred Diary
Ghosts
The Heart of the Family
Never Mind the Reversing Ducks
Nothing but the Truth
The Sacred Diaries of Adrian, Andromeda and Leonard
Stress Family Robinson
Stress Family Robinson 2: The Birthday Party
The Visit
Why I Follow Jesus
You Say Tomato (with Paul McCusker)

ADRIAN PLASS

And
JESUS
will be born

A Collection of
Christmas Poems,
Stories and
Reflections

ILLUSTRATED BY BEN ECCLESTONE

Zondervan

Grand Rapids, Michigan 49530 USA

Zondervan

And Jesus Will Be Born
Copyright © 2003 by Adrian Plass

Illustrations copyright © 2003 by Zondervan

Adrian Plass asserts the moral right to be identified as the author of this work.

Requests for information should be addressed to:

Zondervan, *Grand Rapids, Michigan 49530*

Library of Congress Cataloging-in-Publication Data

Plass, Adrian.
    And Jesus will be born : a collection of Christmas poems, stories, and reflections / Adrian Plass.—1st ed.
        p. cm.
    0-00-713052-X (pbk) ISBN 0-00-713051-1
    1. Christmas. I. Title.
BV45.P58 2003
242'.335 — dc21

                                                                    2003004950

Interior design by Susan Ambs

Illustrations by Ben Ecclestone

Printed in the United States of America

03 04 05 06 07 08 09 /❖ DC/ 10 9 8 7 6 5 4 3 2 1

This book is dedicated to
Tommy and Ellie McCusker,
in the sincere hope that Christmas
will always be wonderful for them

Contents

Introduction: Desirable Nonsense

This mixture of fact and fiction, poetry and prose, reflection and recollection, all on the subject of Christmas, is for you, whoever you are. I do hope you enjoy it. Having said that I have to confess that this particular yearly celebration brings its own problems as far as I am concerned.

The question is, do I actually enjoy Christmas? Well, part of me dreads it – mainly, I suppose, because many of my childhood Christmases were so packed with family conflict that I never quite dared to relax. I loved the stockings and the presents and the decorations and the special food when I was little, but as the years went by I developed a habit of fearing failure on the very day that is supposed to be such a happy one. Trivial arguments over who was going to have which bit of the turkey would turn into crashing, shouting, ragged chaos, followed by sulking on the part of those who favoured that particular strategy, moaning resentment from those who hadn't got what they wanted, and infuriating chewing noises from those who had. Something always seemed to go wrong.

That dark shadow of dread anticipation still creeps over me each year – I think it always will to an extent – but three things have brought a lot of happiness back into Christmas for me. The first is my own children. There are four of them now, their ages ranging from twenty-eight to fifteen, and I shall never forget how Christmas suddenly came alive again for me when Matthew, the oldest, was a small child. Through his eyes I saw the way in which the season shone, and I felt an echo of his excitement in my own heart for the first time in many years. Sometimes I think the only reason that we went on having children was to ensure that there would always be a small one available to enhance Christmas for us!

The second aid to my rediscovery of Christmas is the fact that December the twenty-fifth is the birthday of someone very special – my wife. You thought I was going to say Jesus, didn't you? Yes you did! When Bridget was a girl her parents appointed a day in June to be her official birthday – rather like the queen of England. Nowadays, though, she receives birthday cards, birthday presents, Christmas cards, and Christmas presents all on the same day. Bridget likes Christmas, and she's very good at it, if you know what I mean.

Yes, all right – the third thing is that it's Jesus' birthday as well. And why not? He gave me the children that have brought Christmas alive again for me, and he gave me the wife who has been my closest friend for more than thirty years. I'm sure he hates the shadows that defeat so many of us, and I know he joins us in the life-long battle to let the light in so that they can be dispelled. Our family and the family of the church will be together for ever because of him, even if we die. A nonsense to those of you who do not follow Jesus? Perhaps – but highly desirable nonsense, don't you think?

Happy birthday, Jesus – and thank you.

Happy birthday and Christmas, Bridget.

Happy Christmas to all who read these words.

Part One

THE PROMISE OF CHRISTMAS

I suspect that those of you who do not find this time of year easy will appreciate the poem that follows. Promises are not always kept on this side of the grave. That is the way life is. God will always keep his promises, though, and when we do finally reach heaven, we will be amazed to find that the essence of all the innocent things that we loved most in this world are there. How could that not be so? He made them.

Christmas in Heaven

When I'm in heaven
Tell me there'll be kites to fly,
The kind they say you can control
Although I never did for long,
The kind that spin and spin and spin and spin
Then sulk and dive and die,
And rise again and spin again,
And dive and die and rise up yet again,
I love those kites.

When I'm in heaven
Tell me there'll be friends to meet,
In ancient oak-beamed Sussex pubs
Enfolded by the wanton Downs,
And summer evenings lapping lazily against the shore
Of sweet familiar little lands
Inhabited by silence or by nonsenses,
The things you cannot safely say in any other place,
I love those times.

When I'm in heaven
Tell me there'll be seasons when the colours fly,
Poppies splashing flame
Through dying yellow, living green,
And autumn's burning sadness that has always made me cry
For things that have to end.
For winter fires that blaze like captive suns
But look so cold when morning comes.
I love the way the seasons change.

When I'm in heaven
Tell me there'll be peace at last,
That in some meadow filled with sunshine
Filled with buttercups and filled with friends
You'll chew a straw and fill us in on how things really are,
And if there is some harm in laying earthly hope at heaven's
 door,
Or in this saying so,
Have mercy on my foolishness, dear Lord,
I love this world you made – it's all I know.

When I'm in heaven
Tell me there'll be Christmases without the pain
No memories that will not fade
No chilled and sullen sense of loss
That cannot face the festive flame
Nor breathe excitement from the ice-cream air
Tell me how the things that Christmas should have been
Will be there for eternity in one long shining dawn
For all of us to share
I love the promises of Christmas.

Part Two

PLASS FAMILY CHRISTMAS

Since Bridget and I married in 1970 we have celebrated Christmas together on thirty-two occasions. Since 1974 our children have been added one by one to the mix. It has been good and not so good and just about everything in between. Here are some true accounts of Christmas events and experiences in the world of the Plasses.

Christmas Cards

Why is nothing ever straightforward?

Take Christmas cards, for instance. What could be simpler than writing nice messages on attractive cards and sending them to people who are important in your life? Well, in the Plass household, we have managed to make a mess of even this idiot-proof activity.

Take the year, for instance, when we decided to change our address book about a month before Christmas.

Address books generally survive for about eighteen months in our house, two years if they're lucky. After that length of time they will have become ragged, ketchup-stained, scribbled-on, exhausted versions of their former selves. The cover will have come off, and it will be the cover that one of us will invariably find when we are searching for the book, and then we will get cross and rave about the house and demand to know why nothing is ever in the place where it ought to be and then remember that it was we ourselves who took it out in the car for some insane reason and left it there and have to go and get it and feel stupid.

Anyway, on this occasion we bought a new book in November, and, most unusually, one of us sat down almost immediately and copied out all the addresses and telephone numbers right through from "A" to "P". This would have been fine, except that the following dialogue occurred later on that same day.

ONE OF US: Oh, by the way, I spent this morning copying stuff from the old address book into the new one.

ANOTHER OF US: Oh, well done, that's great.

What a shame "one of us" failed to mention to "another of us" the crucial fact that the copying out had only got as far as "P", because a little later in the day "another of us", thinking that it was no longer needed, took it upon himself to dump the old book in the dustbin, which was, in its turn, emptied the very next morning. You will not be surprised to hear that fairly harsh words passed between "one of us" and "another of us" after that.

All our friends whose names began with anything from "A" to "P" got Christmas cards from us that year. Most of the rest did not. In idle moments I have sometimes pictured most of the rest getting together to gloomily compare notes, to discuss and puzzle over the inexplicable mania that drove Adrian and Bridget Plass, during Advent of all times, to coldly reject the majority of their friends whose surnames began with anything from "Q" to "Z". Why, why, why?

Please, if any of you late alphabet people are reading this now, forgive us for what happened that year. We love you – we do really!

Winter Holiday in Cornwall

I wish I was my son again,
The first in all the world to know,
The cornflake crunch of frosted grass,
Beside the polar paving stones,
Beneath the drip of liquid light,
From water-colour, winter suns.

God really brought me down to earth once. He's rather good at
that sort of thing.

We'd gone to Cornwall for a pre-Christmas holiday, something that we'd always yearned to do as a family. It was early December, bitingly cold, but brilliantly lit by one of those water-colour winter suns that seem to drip liquid light through the atmosphere. Our little white rented cottage overlooked an indescribably beautiful part of the northern coast. That coast must have been planned, built, and illuminated by a creator with time on his hands and a fine, excited eye for detail.

One morning, after a long, lingering, excessive breakfast, we all dressed in layer upon layer of the warmest clothes we could find, and set off, a procession of human barrels, to go for a walk in the ice-cream air. We went a new way. Through a white farm gate and across an expanse of wind-flattened, metallic green grass, towards what looked like a cliff edge a few hundred yards away. Beyond that the sea stretched away for ever, merging with the sky in the strange pale distance.

I walked with Matthew, aged eight, whose every utterance at that time began with an interrogative. My wife, Bridget, strolled beside four-year-old Joseph, deep and thoughtful beyond his years. The smallest barrel, David, aged two, ran ahead of us chuckling delightedly, applauding the seagulls who keeled around us for a few minutes, performing impossible aerobatics with casual vanity.

As we neared the edge of the cliff, I reflected on the fact that we were happy – all of us. We are a close family, but it didn't often happen that we all achieved contentment, all at the same time, when we were all together. You have to work hard to keep a family of five reasonably happy. It's like the circus act where all those plates are kept spinning on the top of tall, thin sticks by someone rushing from one to the other at great speed. The difference with a family is that you never get a chance to stop and take a bow. You just carry on, and get tired. Holidays had always been an opportunity for Bridget and myself to enjoy an awareness of our whole selves, and to give some thought to what we needed to keep our plates spinning.

We had reached the edge. Far beneath us, enclosed by a horse-shoe of unscaleable cliffs, lay one of the most magically secluded bays I had ever seen. Perfect shape, perfect sea, perfect sand, perfect rock pools. There was no way down. We could never use it. We could only look at it. It was as though one of God's successful creation prototypes had been overlooked when the workbench was cleared.

I forgot everything else as I gazed out over this hidden corner of the world. I felt a sudden surge of pride about belonging to the same world as the vast shining sea, the blue-white wash of the sky, and the massive, granulated bulk of the cliffs. These, surely, were symbols of God. Huge, beautiful, sublime, desirable, yet impossible to contain or define narrowly. I was lost in wonder. . . .

"Daddy, want to go loo, daddy!"

My youngest son's voice arrived in my consciousness with urgent haste. David's little face was strained with the knowledge that disaster was imminent. As I struggled to reduce his Michelin-like proportions to an appropriate state of undress, I spoke to God in my mind with some truculence.

"Goodness knows," I complained, "I get little enough time as it is to actually relax and enjoy beautiful things. Why should I have to come down from where I was to cope with little problems like this?"

"I did," said God.

Katy and the
Wicked Witch of the West

Pantomime seems to be a peculiarly British institution. It happens in theatres and halls all over the British Isles at Christmas time and is basically a dramatic performance based on a fairy tale, with music, topical jokes, and lots of interaction between actors and audience. The *Wizard of Oz* is not really a fairy tale, but no one in this country would be very bothered about that. This was Katy's first experience of the phenomenon.

I took little Katy to a show performed in a nearby hall by a local amateur dramatic society. This year the special attraction for children was an afternoon performance of *The Wizard of Oz*. Katy was excited and a little bit scared. She knew the story well and liked all the characters except one, the Wicked Witch of the West. This was the character who had sent her scurrying to safety behind an armchair when the story appeared on television in cartoon form. Like most children of her age, Katy (she prefers "Kate" now that she has turned thirteen) was not yet able to separate fact from fantasy in some areas.

Now, as I dressed her in woollies, ready to walk down the road to this live presentation, she tried to reassure herself.

"Daddy," she said solemnly, "there won't be a Wicked Witch of the West this time, will there? Eh, daddy?"

"Well, I think there will be, darling," I admitted, "but why don't we think of something to say to her when she comes on, so that we won't be scared?"

Katy considered this suggestion seriously for a moment, her brows knitted in concentration. Then her face cleared, "I know what we'll do," she said brightly, "why don't we just say 'One – two – three – BOO!' when we see her, then we'll probably be all right, won't we?"

"Sounds good to me, Katy," I replied. "Let's just practise a few times before we go."

A little later, word perfect in our defensive ploy, we set off in the exciting darkness to walk to the hall, Katy still whispering "One – two – three – BOO!" at intervals, just in case the witch might be hiding behind a garden hedge or in the branches of an overhanging tree.

The inside of the hall, when we arrived, was filled with light and noise, lots and lots of children laughing and chattering with their mums and dads. Such a cheerful atmosphere was it that Katy forgot all her earlier fears as she gossiped with acquaintances and contemporaries.

At last, the lights dimmed, the curtains opened, and the show began.

Katy loved it. She pointed everything out to me as if I was blind. There was the little girl called Dorothy, and there, a little later, was the scarecrow, then the tin man, and finally the lion (the "nice" lion, as Katy hastened to point out). So far, so good, but eventually there came the inevitable moment when a green spotlight was switched on and the wicked witch appeared, cackling horribly, her long bent nose almost touching her long, bent, wart-covered chin.

Amateur dramatic societies are not always able to produce convincing portrayals of benevolent or morally neutral characters, but when it comes to evil caricatures they really go to town. They did on this occasion. This witch was very unpleasant indeed.

Katy was terrified. Forgetting all about "One – two – three – BOO!", she dived under my overcoat and pressed against my chest as if she was trying to get right inside my rib-cage. Nothing I could say or do would persuade her to come out until it was absolutely guaranteed that the witch would not reappear.

Later, after the show, she treated my explanation that the witch was just an ordinary lady dressed up with the scorn that it deserved. An ordinary lady is an ordinary lady – a witch is a witch. Silly Daddy!

I wondered, as we arrived home, if it had been a mistake to take Katy at all, but already, as her coat was being removed, she was telling her mum all about the entertainment with great animation. Clearly, the fear was a part of the whole experience and probably wouldn't do her any harm.

Looking at my daughter a little later as she tucked into her fish-fingers and baked beans, I thought about *The Wizard of Oz*, and how the story closely reflects what I want for Katy and what God has always wanted for each of us.

Like the scarecrow, I want her to have a brain that is creative and strong. I would like her to have a heart that is generous and loving, like the tin man. And, of course, I hope she will be as brave as a lion, especially when the wicked witches of this world appear. I'm sure she'll find something more effective than "One – two – three – BOO!" with which to defend herself.

Most of all, perhaps, I would like Katy to carry through life the same urgent and excited desire as Dorothy (and, incidentally, the prodigal son); and that is, quite simply, a yearning, in the end, to go home.

Getting What You Want?

I once made the mistake of telling one of my own children how I went about persuading my parents to buy me a particular book that I wanted.

I explained that I had read all of a certain series of books by Enid Blyton (that terrible writer whose books are mysteriously enjoyed by generation after generation of children who stubbornly refuse not to like them), and that I now desperately wanted the latest in the series, a book entitled *The River of Adventure*. Neither Christmas nor my birthday were in sight, and as my parents were not very well off, I was well aware that seven and sixpence was far more money than they would care to part with, especially as the book was bound to appear in the library eventually anyway. But I was merciless. I embarked on a callous, long-term campaign that simply involved saying the words *River of Adventure* over and over again, the theory being that eventually my parents would crack under the pressure and I would get my book.

"River of Adventure – River of Adventure – River of Adventure – River of Adventure – River of Adventure ..."

Those were the words that began to drive my mother and father mad over the weeks that followed. I was as stubborn at the age of ten as I sometimes can be now, and I WANTED THAT BOOK. I was determined to go on repeating the phrase until my mission was accomplished, and nothing was going to stop me. Looking back, I find it interesting to reflect on the stages that my poor parents went through in their response to this ploy. They were mildly amused at first, perhaps thinking my insistence rather touching, but that phase soon passed. Their amusement turned swiftly to irritation as they discovered that their every waking hour in my presence was filled with the same phrase, accompanying all else that happened, like the bassline of a track being played on someone else's hi-fi in the next room.

Irritation was followed by downright anger and threats, all of which failed to stem or even briefly interrupt my flow, the content of which had, by now, resolved itself into a sort of condensed version of the original.

"Riverererventure – Riverererventure – Riverererventure – Riverererventure – Riverererventure ..."

They never really stood a chance, did they? But they did try everything. They ignored me.

I went on saying it.

They talked reasonably to me.

I went on saying it.

They made promises for the distant future.

I went on saying it.

They told me in serious, end-of-our-tether tones that enough was enough.

I went on saying it.

"Riverererventure – Riverererventure – Riverererventure – Riverererventure – Riverererventure . . ."

Finally, wild-eyed, haggard, and defeated, they bought me the book. It was one of the few victories in a not very victorious childhood.

When, some years ago, I told one of my sons this story, he listened with enormous interest, then gazed speculatively at me for a moment.

"Nintendo," he said. "Nintendo – Nintendo – Nintendo – Nintendo . . ."

Bringing Christmas Home from Germany

I have a stubborn streak.

My mother told Bridget and me that when I was a very small child she sometimes had to drag me along the High Street of the village where we lived, screaming like a banshee because I hadn't been allowed to have my own way. My wife feels that this scenario was prophetic.

I have described elsewhere one of the occasions when my stubborn spirit became horribly evident.

It happened shortly after the death of my grandmother, when I walked nine miles from my home in Rusthall to a town five miles from the village where my grandmother had lived, and then back again. I was seven years old. Something in me needed to go to the place where Nanna had lived to check that this fabled state of death was a hard fact. Five miles from her house I suddenly realised that I was wasting my time because she would not be there. I turned for home. The police, called by my parents when I was nowhere to be found much earlier that day, had been scouring the countryside around Rusthall for hours. I explained patiently to them and to my parents that I had told them exactly where I was going. Had they not believed me?

This stubborn tendency has continued throughout my adult life, manifesting itself in some unexpected areas, one of these being the bringing home of awkward or inappropriate objects from foreign parts on aeroplanes. A couple of examples.

We were presented with a very large didgeridoo during our first trip to Australia, but we then had to fly to New Zealand for a conference before returning home. Landing in Auckland, we were informed by a customs official that the didgeridoo, made, as I am sure you know, by hollowing out a specially selected branch of a tree, was a vegetable in the technical sense and could not therefore be permitted into the country. A ludicrous discussion then developed.

I asked if a table was a vegetable and therefore not admissible. What about a pencil? A pencil was just as much a hollowed out length of wood as a didgeridoo, wasn't it? Supposing I had a violin in my luggage, or a clarinet, or a bassoon, or a recorder, or a cello, or a double bass? What then? When you came to think about it, I suggested, the luggage of an orchestra travelling by plane was actually nothing more than a load of strangely shaped vegetables, wasn't it? Would they be refused entry for the same reason? When did a vegetable stop being a vegetable and become the thing that it had been made into? Wasn't that, I queried politely, the question that really needed to be asked and answered?

Pale, weary, and running out of arguments, the customs official agreed at last that I could take my didgeridoo into and out of New Zealand as long as it was wrapped up securely from end to end and remained so wrapped throughout the trip. I agreed. My didgeridoo is now standing in the corner of our living-room next to the piano. I'm glad I brought it back all this way, and it is very ornamental, but I still haven't learned how to play it. . . .

Then there is our Bangladeshi harmonium. That sits in another corner of the room, just by the window.

In the course of a trip that Bridget and I made to Bangladesh in January 2000, we noticed this instrument being played in a number of settings, including church services, where it was used to accompany hymns or choruses. Basically, it is a wooden box about the size of a small suitcase, made from highly polished Burmese teak. With the left hand air is pushed through the instrument by means of a hinged, bellows-like arrangement at the back, while the melody is played with the other hand on a short, traditional keyboard at the front. As with an organ there are various stops that can be pulled out or pushed in to change the pitch or tone.

Towards the end of our stay we became very conscious that, apart from a selection of amazingly cheap and glowingly beautiful coloured saris, we had bought nothing that was essentially Bangladeshi to remind us of our trip in the future. Then, as we were strolling through the narrow streets of the Hindu quarter of Dhaka, we came across a shop where these very attractive harmoniums were being made and sold. It was then that the old madness came over me. Why should we not take one of these instruments back to England on the plane with us? The answer to that question was, of course, very simple. We should not take one because it would be very fragile, quite heavy, and extremely awkward to deal with at both ends of the flight. Apart from anything else, it was quite possible that it might not survive the journey at all.

And so, of course, we had to have it.

The men who worked in the shop took hours making sure that the one we selected was perfectly in tune and then very helpfully found a wooden box in which to pack our new possession for its long journey. Apart from a brief battle at the airport when it was suggested that the box should go into the hold with all the other luggage (oh, no!), we experienced very few problems in transporting our little bit of a far country back home to East Sussex. One tiny piece of wood was slightly chipped away from the base, but that was easily glued, and now our Bangladeshi harmonium is here, and we are glad, although I still haven't learned how to play it. . . .

The piece of Germany that I was determined to bring home has become one of our great delights.

It was at the end of November 1999 that I found myself in the hilly but charming old East German town of Annaberg-Buchholz with Christian Rendell, who is my friend, translator, and interpreter. We were nearing the end of a nine-day speaking tour that had taken us from one side of Germany to the other. Christian was especially pleased to have arrived in this part of the world because he was planning to buy a typically German item of Christmas decoration.

"I want to buy a really nice Weihnachts pyramide," he explained, "and this is the centre of the area where they are made."

As I wasn't altogether sure what he was talking about I didn't take a great deal of notice, but I was more than happy to join him as we looked around the colourful, traditional Christmas market that had been set up on the central square of Annaberg-Buchholz. At last, in a small stall at the other end of the market we found an example of what Christian was looking for. I was enchanted. On a pyramid of circular platforms, angels and nativity figures revolved slowly when candles were lit in little holders attached to the base of the object. Every part of the object was beautifully carved and very delicately constructed. This was a rather small example, though, and the man in charge of the stall was unable to take credit cards. However, he informed us, the main shop was in a street only a short distance away. We should try there. We did, and in that shop we found Weihnachts pyramides of every size and degree of ornamentation, some in plain wood and some painted. They were magnificent, and – yes, you guessed it – I had to have one.

The medium-sized example that I chose was still large enough to be a bit of a nuisance. It fitted nicely into its own box when some of the parts had been removed and packed with the rest, but I knew that, because of its fragility, I would have to carefully nurse my new baby through the forthcoming flight to England. It was also very expensive. I held my breath as the lady behind the counter ran my credit-card number through her machine (I wasn't sure how much credit I had left!), and then, suddenly, it was mine.

I cannot tell you what a pleasure it was to produce this purchase when I returned home. I made sure that Bridget saw it in all its glory, assembled and lit, before I told her how much it cost, and by then she was too smitten to care.

It was a mad thing to do really, but I have a feeling that our Weihnachts pyramide is going to become one of our favourite decorations when we take it down from the loft at Christmas time each year. Apart from anything else, it will always remind me of Germany and of all the friends I have made and met since I first started visiting that country nearly a decade ago. That makes it very special.

Determination works sometimes. The determination of God to enter into this world as a little baby is a good example. He got very nastily knocked about in the course of his journey, but he reached the place where he wanted and needed to be in the end, and because of that, thank God, so will we.

The Boy in the Box

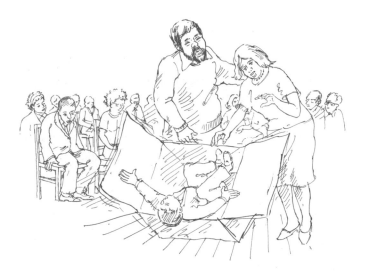

There is one very obvious problem with simple plans. They can only get more complicated. Let me offer you an example that is burned onto my memory like a brand on the hide of a cow (or bull – mustn't be sexist).

Bridget and I had been asked to do the talk for the Christmas Day service at our church. After much discussion we decided to make the central point that God's most special and valuable presents to us might turn out to be things that we already had, such as our children. But how were we to convey this idea in a dramatic and memorable way? Something vivid and immediate was required.

"Why don't we get a large box," suggested Bridget, "and hide David in it before the service begins. We can wrap it in Christmas paper and put a ribbon round it and all that, and then when we come to the right bit of the talk we'll open it up and David can come leaping out and be the special present we were talking about. What do you think?"

I thought it was an excellent idea. David was our youngest son, a very sweet little boy of seven, whose only serious character flaw was a terribly bad temper that tended to erupt whenever he felt that some great injustice had been done to him. David was the only child we knew who had been thrown out of his own birthday party by his own parents for at least two years running. For the purposes of our talk he was just a little unpredictable, but, crucially, the right size.

Everything went according to plan, right up to the point when we were just about to leave the house for church on Christmas morning. David had agreed to be the boy in the box, the box was made and wrapped and beribboned, our talk was as planned as our talks ever get, and we were leaving in time to set it all up before anyone else appeared.

At the last moment David bottled out. He wasn't going to do it, and we couldn't make him do it. He didn't want to get in that box and then jump out in front of all those people and feel silly and that was all there was to it. We couldn't blame him really. It was a big thing to ask, and anyway, we didn't want David exploding like a little firecracker for the rest of Christmas Day, so we asked Joe, aged nine, if he would do it instead.

Joe has always been and still is a very obliging fellow.

"Oh, yes," he said when we tentatively asked him, "I'll do it."

We arrived at the church and unloaded the car, then we helped him climb into the box. It was not easy. There had only just been enough room for David, and Joe was quite a bit taller and wider than his little brother. We did manage to get the cardboard container closed down, though, and, after reminding its occupant that he must not make a sound or move a muscle until the right time, we went on with our preparations for the service.

What was it that made this Christmas service so very much longer than usual? Was it the number of children who came up the front to show everyone what Father Christmas had brought them? Was it the inclusion of all those extra Christmas-related poems and bits and pieces that creep into such services? Whatever the reason, it must have been very nearly three-quarters of an hour before the moment scheduled for Joe's dramatic emergence arrived.

"Now let's open this great big present," I declared, "and when we do, I think we'll find that one of God's best presents of all to Bridget and I will be inside."

As I pulled on the knot in the ribbon, the children on the front row leaned forward. All presents, even other people's, were so exciting! I lifted the lid of the box and stood back. Nothing happened. Where was the boy leaping to his feet as a surprise to everybody? Where was our visual aid? I stepped forward and peered into the container. As I did so, Joe's arms flailed into view, only to slump and hang heavily over the edge of the box, as if he was an exhausted swimmer who had finally reached dry land. The effort of doing this tilted the box forward towards the congregation, tipping our middle son out in a crumpled heap onto the carpet. White-faced and gasping for breath, Joe managed to lurch and stumble his way down the centre aisle and out through the double doors at the back towards the blessed open air of the car-park.

The children on the front row were looking puzzled. Why was God's best present of all to Bridget and me a pallid, suffocating boy? The adults looked concerned and very faintly censorious. Fancy shutting a boy up in a tiny, airless space like that, just to make a point!

"So," I concluded feebly, "there we are. As I said, the best gifts are often the ones we've already got."

With that, Bridget and me collected our notes and our box and our remaining dignity and hurried down the aisle towards the double doors, anxious to check on the condition of our poor asphyxiated son.

Interestingly, the Plass family were the first ones away from church on that particular Christmas morning. . . .

Katy Plass, Christmas, and the Billions of Plates

As a little girl, our daughter Kate always loved everything to do with Christmas. She still does, but in those early years each shining area of activity connected with the Advent season filled her with a quite breathless excitement and anticipation.

Choosing a Christmas tree from hundreds of possible candidates at one of our local garden centres was a special favourite. The Spruce Pine that had unquestionably been ordained before the beginning of time to grace our home on this occasion had to be exactly right. It must not be too overbearingly tall nor too ridiculously short. It must have an even and symmetrical shape like a girl curtseying in an old-fashioned party frock, with a clerk bit at the top for the angel, and not be disguising a significant list to port that you didn't notice until you got it home and stood it in its pot. Although we felt a warm and sorrowful sympathy with disabled Christmas trees, we had no wish to adopt one. Our tree must be green and bushy, but not so bushy that it stuck right out into the centre of our quite small sitting-room. Trees that made the foolish mistake of taking up too much space in this way were likely to find their lower branches under constant attack from the muscular gyrations of the tail that was immovably attached to one end of our large, black, hairy dog.

"Oh, Rosie – for goodness *sake!*" three of us would shriek more or less in unison as yet another coloured-glass, dangling thing got batted into the air, often splintering to its tinkling death on the wall or against the stone surround of the fireplace. Poor Rosie would pant and grin and look from one to the other of us in bewilderment, wondering why she was being told off for demonstrating her good will. Then, suddenly inspired, she would leap about the room and wag her tail with even more devastating vigour in case the problem was that we hadn't noticed that clear gesture of friendship in the first place.

Once the tree had been brought home and secured in its pot with earth and stones and old bits of brick and a few snails and worms, it had to be decorated. Katy loved doing this as well. Always, always, always, though, we had a problem with the Christmas tree lights, and herein lies one of the great mysteries with which it seems that mankind is doomed to wrestle eternally.

It is this. Every year, as the Christmas celebrations came to an end, we would religiously take all the lengths of purple and silver tinsel, all the coloured glass decorations that had survived Rosie's tail, all the wonderful, funny little oddments made by the children over the years, and all the electric lights that had winked and sparkled their way through the season, and we would place them with enormous care in boxes clearly labelled on the top with orange felt-pen to show that they must not be touched until next year.

Just before putting the lid on the box that contained the neatly coiled, plastic-covered flex to which the tree lights were attached, we always plugged them into a socket on an extension lead, simply to check that the process of removing them from the tree had not caused any damage. Observing the glowing nest of light in the bottom of the container with childish satisfaction, we would switch off, unplug, place the lid firmly on top of the box, and bear it away with sacramental horizontality to be placed with all the other boxes of decorations in some remote corner of the loft where there was no reason for anyone to go for any other purpose.

Now, here is the mystery.

Eleven and a half months after this fastidious storage exercise, the new tree, succulent, symmetrical, green and naked, would be ready and waiting in its place, branches stretched wide, waiting like a bride to be dressed. One of us would be deputed to ascend to the loft in order to bring down those carefully packed boxes so that the simple joy of tree decoration could begin.

"After all," we carolled to each other with brittle optimism as we waited for the elected one to return, "we put everything away really carefully in January, didn't we? And no one's touched any of it since then, so we know the lights are working and we can just take the rest of the stuff out and – well, get on with it ..."

"Quite!" Nods and smiles would bob brightly around among us as we tried to stifle the dread that each of us felt in our heart of hearts.

When the boxes appeared we would examine them and discover that, yet again, a man had crept into our loft at some point during the year when we were all out, with the sole and malicious intention of messing up our Christmas things. What a horrible, unrepentant Scrooge of a man he must have been, a hater of all things Christmassy. He had left at least one of the lids half off a box (we clearly remembered closing each one extremely carefully). He had broken two or three of the glass ornaments. It must have been him because we all recalled how adamant we had been that only complete ones should be stored in the boxes. Our neatly folded silver and purple tinsel he had taken out, shaken violently (probably in his teeth), tied it all into knots, and then stirred it about in some dust he had brought with him specially for the purpose, so that it no longer looked as shiny and glittery as it had done eleven months ago. Some of the prettiest things, items that one or more of us were prepared to swear on our mothers' graves had definitely been packed away with the rest, had just gone. He had stolen them.

Worst of all, we would discover that he had taken the neat coil of flex to which our Christmas tree lights were attached, and tied knots in that also in three different places, and made a fault happen in the wiring so that the bulbs didn't light up any more, which meant that the least practical person in the house would end up insisting on spending hours trying to mend them despite having lost his glasses, and he would get hot and cross and start to see double and say rude things and give up and send someone down to the shop to buy a new set.

At last all these problems would be sorted out, and sure enough, the old magic would happen just as it had happened the year before and the year before that and for as long as the younger members of the family could remember. Our tree, the final and visible guarantee that Christmas really was going to happen yet again, stood dark and blazing in the corner of the room like an enormous velvet-shrouded jewel that we had forgotten we could afford, making us feel like millionaires who have blown all their money on one thing but consider it well spent.

Choosing, wrapping, and labelling presents for Bridget and me and her three big brothers was another seasonal task that Katy enjoyed. Bridget and I always preferred it when she wrote us a story or drew us a picture, but, innocent of such crass, grown-up concepts as commercialism, she loved involvement in the urgency and anticipation of the annual shopping surge that floods through this country each year in the two or three weeks before Christmas. Best of all was arriving home with her purchases, necessarily humble given her slender resources, but vastly more valuable than the most precious rubies or diamonds because of the love which had been poured into their selection.

Breathless and tense with excitement she would wrap and label her gifts with horribly sticky, inexpert assistance from me, or highly competent, non-messy assistance from Bridget, and bear them away to be placed on the ever-growing pile of presents beneath our glittering tree. Every now and then in the course of the day she would flitter back into the living-room to pat them gently or rearrange them or hint shamelessly to her brothers about what they might contain or simply look at them and hug herself with delight.

But Father Christmas was easily the best thing of all, as far as Katy was concerned. In case this book should reach some far-flung part of the world where that gentleman is not known, let me quickly explain who he is.

Father Christmas is a fat, jolly man dressed in red jacket and trousers trimmed with white fur. He wears black boots and a floppy pointed hat with what looks like a snowball on the end. His hair and his big bushy beard are also as white as snow, and he carries a big sack over his shoulder, full of presents for good children and, although I imagine he is unaware of this, bribes for not-so-good children. He lives somewhere in the far north, perhaps Greenland, in a place where elves and fairies work hard all year to make toys for the following December. On Christmas Eve Father Christmas loads up his sleigh with bulging sacks and sets off through the sky, pulled by flying reindeer, to take presents to children all over the world. Given that his preferred method of entry is down through the chimney, we must suppose that the widespread adoption of central heating has caused him some problems, but we have to remember that Father Christmas is extremely ingenious.

In England all the children hang stockings or pillowcases (times have changed) at the ends of their beds before they go to sleep, hoping, usually with justification, that the morning will find them filled with gifts.

I remember myself, as a small child, the experience of waking at some ridiculously early hour on Christmas morning, sitting up, and reaching a hand out in the darkness towards the bottom of my bed, anxious to know if "HE" had been. The thrill when that urgently questing hand came into contact with the weighty bulkiness of my newly-filled pillowcase and the intriguing shapes of individual gifts has probably not been equalled, and certainly not exceeded, by any other event or adventure in my life. It was the purest form of magic.

Katy was just the same. Bridget and I counted ourselves lucky if we ever managed to sleep past five-thirty on the morning of Christmas

Day. At about that time a small figure in an even smaller night-dress, quivering with joy, would invariably appear in the doorway of our bedroom, hauling her loaded pillowcase along the floor behind her and squeaking excitedly, "Mummy! Daddy! He's been! Look, he's been!"

Katy's next, vigorously decisive move would be to drag her three big, occasionally hungover brothers out of bed and down the stairs with *their* pillowcases so that we could all assemble in the sitting-room, bleary-eyed, strangely dressed, but determinedly festive, to unwrap the gifts that Father Christmas had left. Soon we would be sitting in a sea of crumpled, coloured paper, looking covetously at other people's presents and parrying Katy's puzzled queries about why Father Christmas had put Woolworth's price tags on some of the things he had brought from his workshop in Greenland. It was – still is – great fun.

Even more puzzling and intriguing for Katy was the business of the billions of plates.

A further tradition maintained in many homes in this part of the world is that of leaving a mince-pie and a glass of sherry for Father Christmas to eat and drink in the course of his unremittingly busy night. Accordingly, Katy, a stern traditionalist like all healthy children, insisted that these refreshments should be left on a chair or a shelf in her room every Christmas Eve. She must have felt her insistence to be fully justified by the fact that *all* the sherry (how can you disappoint a child?) and at least part of the mince-pie would invariably have been consumed by the time she woke up in the morning. This was fine, but the phenomenon she wrestled with one Christmas morning was the disappearance of the plate on which the mince-pie had been standing. The empty sherry glass was there, slightly less than half the pie and a trickle of crumbs remained on the chair by her bed, but of the plate there was no trace.

Four-year-old children are interestingly selective when it comes to what is credible and what is definitely not. Clearly Katy had no problems with the perfectly reasonable proposition that Father Christmas must be lurching through the night sky in a state of terminal, bloated drunkenness with a million mince-pies and countless gallons of sherry sloshing around inside him, nor with the logistical difficulties that must arise in planning to visit all the homes in the world in one night, but the idea of him removing plates from every house he visited and taking them all back to Greenland was a matter for headshaking wonder.

There must be billions of them! What did he *do* with them all? Grandma had a wooden dresser with plates standing in a row, but only about four or five. Greenland must be full of dressers – in fact, Greenland must be mainly dressers. Rows and rows of dressers full of plates that used to have mince-pies on them, stretching off into the distance as far as the eye could see. Nothing but dressers and plates all over Greenland. Father Christmas must *really* like plates. . . .

By next Christmas Kate will be nudging fourteen. She is still a delight, and as a family we shall enjoy Christmas as we have always done, but there will be no very little ones to give the season the kind of sparkle that is their very special gift to the adults who look after them.

Bridget and I know people who find it very hard to contemplate the prospect of becoming grandparents.

We don't.

After the Excess

In this part of the world Christmas is, for better or for worse, traditionally a time for eating too much. I have been wrestling with my weight for years. What follows is a very familiar pattern!

expansion was not good business for my body
then I replaced the four sugars in my tea
with sweeteners no after taste eh funny
fat out fibre shovelled in or through
got a shade depressed a little blue
a friend told me alcohol inflates
gave up claret very nearly died
no more booze nothing fried
full of tuna fish and dates
planned to cheat but then
a miracle I saw my feet
like other better men
fresh air was sweet
and nature smiled
I ran and leapt
soundly slept
happy child
so serene
so lean
a bit
fit
I

ate
a bit
a treat
or trophy
had a steak
a titchy cake
a glass of port
a prize I thought
for dieting so well
oh I smiled as I fell
suddenly wanted chops
crazy eyed I hit the shops
syrup jam and lemon cheese
do spring into my trolley please
doughnuts plumply filled with jam
cover me with sticky sugar here I am
chocolate fancy chocolate milk or plain
make the orbit of my lusting mouth again
crinkly scrummy scrunchy deep fried chips
how I yearn to squeeze you firmly in my lips
expansion was not good business for my body

Part Three

STORY TIME

The tradition of storytelling has made something of a come back in recent years. I do hope that Christians welcome this trend. After all, the tradition was established by a rather crucial contributor to the founding of the Christian faith. Christmas is such a specially good time for stories, don't you think?

The Christmas Visit

The Visit, a collection of six short stories, first appeared in a book called *The Final Boundary* and was later published as a separate, illustrated volume. It describes a visit made by "The Founder" to an ordinary English church, and is told from the point of view of the person who arranges and hosts his visit. The opening story in the original collection begins with the following words:

> Our church used to be very okay. We did all the things that
> churches do just about as well as they could be done, and

we talked about our founder with reverence and proper gratitude. We said how much we would have liked to meet him when he was around and how much we looked forward to seeing him at some remote time in the future. The unexpected news that he was going to pay us an extended visit now, in the present, was, to say the least, very disturbing.

"The Christmas Visit", originally published in Holland, is an additional story that continues the theme.

I was ashamed of Christmas. I didn't want him to see what it had become. What would he do or say when he saw how his birthday was celebrated today? The money, the food, the increasingly expensive gifts, the drunkenness, the forbidden kisses picked up like dirty sweets at office or works parties, the once-a-year bonhomie that was often just a postponement of hostilities; it was all so far removed from the simplicity of his actual birthday, and from the man himself, who regarded all possessions as generous loans from God, to be passed on as soon as possible to someone else in need.

I remembered the incident in the temple all those years ago when he drove the merchants out with strong words and knotted ropes. What might he not do in Oxford Street on Christmas Eve if there was a machine-gun handy? An irrational thought perhaps, but after being with him for only a few months, I realised that it just wasn't possible to predict anything as far as he was concerned. He could be so tender and encouraging with people who, frankly, I thought were horrible or repulsive, and then lay into some quite respectable dignitary as if he was addressing the Devil himself. After only a few incidents of the latter kind, most churches and public institutions stopped inviting him to speak. He was too disruptive, too liable to see through the outside of things and people, too likely to demand that they do something about the real problems that usually remain hidden.

In one place, renowned for lively, dynamic expressions of faith, he turned on the church leaders in front of the congregation and asked them if they didn't think it was about time to wake up. In another, he climbed to the pulpit to speak but broke down as he looked at the people in the pews. His sermon was nothing but tears.

This all sounds very fine, but it wasn't easy for me. More often than not, I was the one who got it in the neck afterwards from outraged or upset church elders – as if I was able to influence him! There were times when I felt quite resentful. Take the Danvers Hall disaster, for instance. He'd been asked to speak there one evening, not long before Christmas. It was absolutely jam-packed, and he'd actually stood up to begin speaking when it happened. Before he could say a word, a little voice rang out from the back of the hall. "Dizzy friend! Dizzy friend! Wanna say 'lo to Dizzy friend!"

I knew that voice. It was Dizzy – short for Desiree, of all things – the little girl with learning difficulties who lived not very far from me. He met her in the street very early on in his stay and had visited her once a week without fail ever since, in the little council flat where she lived with her mother. Dizzy looked rather strange, and she was not very bright, but she adored her weekly visitor and always drew a picture to give him when he came. I didn't always go. I thought the weekly commitment unnecessarily heavy, and also there was something about the way Dizzy looked and behaved that just – well – put me off.

When I heard her voice that evening, my heart sank. It was happening all over again! Why couldn't things go according to plan, just once? Why on earth had Dizzy's mother brought a retarded child to an evening meeting for adults? Surely she must have known that the girl would never stay in her seat once she realised who was standing up at the front.

And that's what happened. Dizzy followed up her shout of joy by scrambling down from her chair and limping confidently up to the front, clutching a crumpled sheet of paper in her hand. When she reached him she stopped dead, and, standing with her heels together and her back straight like a little soldier, she pushed her arm out stiffly towards him, offering him the piece of paper. It was one of her blessed pictures. Leaning forward from my seat on the end of the front row, I could see her face, eyes shining with eager anticipation, tongue extended with the effort of concentration.

He took the paper from her hand, smoothed it out carefully, and examined the picture with enormous gravity, like an art expert with an old master. Finally, he laid the masterpiece down on a small table beside him and turned back to Dizzy, his face breaking into a laughing smile. He threw his arms out to catch her as she jumped excitedly towards him, swinging her high, so that their faces met for the obligatory kiss. She leaned her head back, took his face in her hands, and, gazing fondly at his squashed features, said, "I love you best, I do!"

He hugged her to him, then carried her back down the centre aisle to her mother, whose beam was as broad as Dizzy's. But then, to my horror, he turned to the assembled masses, waved happily a couple of times and disappeared through the exit door at the back. He'd done it again! The organisers descended on me in a body.

Was he coming back? Was he ill? Did he realise how much people had looked forward to his talk? Who did he think he was . . . ?

I answered as best I could, and escaped at last, feeling more than a little peeved by the evening's events.

"They expected to hear a good sermon," I complained later when I saw him.

"They saw a better one," he replied and wouldn't discuss it any more.

Now, it was nearly Christmas, and part of me was dreading what would happen when he took in the reality of what this "Christian" festival had become. Yes – I know he knew everything anyway, but what you have to understand is that he didn't act as though he did. He got angry or sad or amused or encouraged by things and people in the same spontaneous way as anyone else. What would he do when he saw – Christmas?

As it happened, he was so busy locally during the days leading up to Christmas that I began to believe there might not be a problem after all. Then, just before bedtime on the night before Christmas Eve, he yawned, stretched, and informed me that tomorrow was to be the one "day off" he was allowed during his stay.

"What shall we do?" I asked nervously. "Just stay at home quietly, eh? That would be nice."

"No," he said serenely, "you stay at home. I'm going to the National Gallery, I'm going to walk in Hyde Park" – his eyes became dreamy – "I'm going to feed pigeons in Trafalgar Square, I'm going to . . . well, have a day off. Goodnight!"

He was going to London on Christmas Eve! The next day, as I saw him off on the train I thanked my lucky stars that he hadn't wanted me to go with him. Galleries, Hyde Park, pigeons – they were all right, but I didn't want to be there when he wandered into the Devil's fairground that commercial London became at this time of year. I couldn't relax at all that day. It was quite a relief when I heard him come in through the front door. At least he was back. Then I saw him. There was death in his eyes and pain in his body. He walked straight past me and stood, silhouetted, staring out of the window, arms outstretched, hands clamped to the frame on either side, his head tilted on to one shoulder as if its weight had grown too much to bear. He said just five words, but I don't think they were addressed to me particularly.

"What more can I do?"

I must have still been smarting from occasions like the Danvers Hall fiasco. That's the only thing I can think of to explain the unholy relish with which I compounded his unhappiness a minute or two later.

"I hope you haven't forgotten that you said yes to a dinner engagement this evening. You've just got time to change. I don't think I'll come – I'm rather tired."

Turning quickly, I left the room, knowing from experience that if I saw the expression on his face when he turned round to look at me, my sulk would be impossible. I went upstairs and lay on my bed – listening. There was silence for a while, then I heard him come slowly upstairs and move around in his bedroom and the bathroom. Finally, he went down to the hall, and the front door squeaked as it opened. There was a pause, I knew instinctively that it was *my* pause – an invitation to join him after all.

Not joining him – staying where I was, felt like stabbing myself, but for the sake of some strange, masochistic satisfaction, I gritted my teeth and hung on until the front door slammed, and I knew he'd gone. This time, I told myself, I'm not giving in! I'm staying right here until he sees that the way he carries on isn't fair to me, and he's ready to apologise and coax me back into good humour. My mind played pleasantly with the picture of myself, gradually agreeing to be comforted against my better judgement. Yes! That's what I'd do. Just wait here in my room until he saw sense – even if it took all night and all the next day.

I lasted for ten minutes, then I panicked. The petty satisfaction from my little tantrum drained away and left me feeling cold and horribly empty inside.

What had I done? Tomorrow was his birthday, and my gift to him, at a time when he felt injured and vulnerable, had been bad temper and calculated rejection. I caught sight suddenly of my own face in a mirror at the other end of the room. It looked weak and wild and altogether loathsome. A little sob of pure emotion escaped me as I levered myself off the bed and hurried downstairs to the telephone. I'd just check that he was still at this dinner and then join him there. Everything would be all right after all.

I dialled. Someone picked up the phone at the other end. We spoke. It wasn't going to be all right. He wasn't there. He'd arrived, stayed for five minutes, then made his apologies and gone.

"He seemed rather upset," said the voice. "Is there something wrong?"

I put down the phone, unable to answer, and stood for a moment, irresolute. Where would he be likely to go? Him in particular. Where would he go on Christmas Eve? My eye caught the personal phone directory lying on the hall table. That was it! I'd phone every possible place where he might have gone. I did it. I phoned churches and friends and acquaintances, hacking my way crudely through the forest of Christmas greetings without stopping to explain. I would be lucky to have any friends left at all after this. But I couldn't help it; everything in me wanted only to find him, to say sorry to him, to make sure he knew someone wanted him on this night of all nights, despite the glare and coarseness and crudity of the things he'd seen in the city. It was no use. No one had seen him.

Knowing how pointless it was, I put on overcoat and gloves and went out into town to search the streets. I looked everywhere. Everything I saw and heard seemed to be connected in some way with him. Carols playing in late-opening supermarkets, "Away in a Manger" belting out through two huge speakers outside the Parish church on the edge of the town square, and in the church itself, a little flock of women putting some extra Christmas Day touches to a life-size nativity scene at the back of the building. It was nice. He would have liked it. But he wasn't there.

Each pub was a box of noise, overflowing with sound and light as I opened doors and peered hopefully through the haze of cigarette smoke. He *could* have been there. He'd spent hours in pubs over the last few months, talking and laughing with the regulars. But he wasn't there now, he wasn't anywhere that I looked. Doorways, car parks, side streets, odd forgotten corners of the backs of buildings, I explored everywhere that I could think of, and it was all a waste of time. For hours I searched in vain until I was beginning to break up inside. As I began to make my way wearily back in the direction of home, I passed little knots of warmly dressed people stepping out briskly towards the church, happily anticipating the magic of the midnight service. They were looking for him, too, on this special night, and they'd probably find him, long before I did.

I arrived home, hoping against hope that he'd come back while I was out, but I could tell from the silence as I pushed the front door open that the house was empty. It was like a huge dark coffin, and in my misery it seemed to me that I might as well die then and there if I'd lost him for good. I sank to my knees on the hall carpet, unable to hold back the tears any more, stretching my arms out into the darkness like a child lost in the night. Deep inside, a part of me, too small and frail and vulnerable to have risked coming out for years and years, rose through my body and mind with a tumultuous rushing insistence, to emerge as a single desperate cry of "HELP ME!"

Suddenly I knew where he was with absolute certainty; felt, in fact, as if I'd known all along. Minutes later I was standing outside the door of the little flat. I rang the bell, and waited impatiently. Seconds later, the door opened.

"Is he here?" I couldn't have produced small talk if I'd tried.

The woman pointed at the sitting room door, her expression an odd mixture of wonderment and joy. "In there," she whispered. "Go in if you want. They're in there."

Behind the closed door I could hear "Away in a Manger" tinkling from a music-box. As I pushed the door open, the only light in the room, a fat red candle on the upright piano that the little girl loved so much, flickered in the draught and nearly went out.

Dizzy was sitting in an armchair at the side of the room, looking almost beautiful in the half-light. All around her in a wide semi-circle stood her entire collection of soft-toy animals, arranged as though they were watching the figure who reclined peacefully on the floor in front of her chair. As I took my place quietly on the carpet beside the little girl, it seemed to me that she had a new kind of dignity, a special pride that was nothing to do with vanity. As she sat, she gently stroked the head that lay, quite relaxed, against her knee and said softly, over and over again, "Don' cry 'bout Christmas. Don' cry 'bout Christmas."

Sainted Emily's Bicycle
(A Stress Family Robinson Tale)

The Stress Family Robinson books are fictional accounts of the way in which a more-or-less typical Christian English family deals with the collision between faith and real life on a day-to-day basis. The family consists of parents Mike, a calm, kindly, but perhaps slightly unimaginative junior-school headmaster, and his wife, Kathy, an attractive, emotional, generally well-meaning person, who explodes and crumples with rather alarming frequency.

Jack, the oldest child, is warm, witty, and almost a grown-up, though he can revert to more immature behaviour when in conflict with his younger brother Mark.

Mark is a typically self-absorbed teenager, whose life revolves around his friends and his spare-time activities. Mark's untidy, disorganised approach to life infuriates his mother on a regular basis.

Felicity, who tells this story, is the youngest child, a lively, ingenuous lover of life, who adores her brothers and generally manages to deal skilfully with her parents.

Dip is a single and deeply beloved family friend.

My name is Felicity Robinson and I am a ten-year-old girl, thank goodness, having lived in a house with two brothers. I don't mean I don't like my brothers, because I do. I'm just glad I'm a girl. Jack is the oldest. He thinks he is grown-up and is quite funny but not as funny as he thinks he is with long hair tied in a sort of tail, and Mark is the next oldest. He is seventeen. He gets shouted at by Mummy a lot and is supposed to be working to pass some exams. Mummy says there is less chance of this happening than a yeti moving into the shed in our back garden.

Mummy is called Kathy. She is dark and loud and supposed to be good-looking and she used to be a writer before we came along and spoiled it. She talks a lot and cries quite a bit and ends up saying sorry more than anyone else in our family. She thinks Jack is grown up as well. They have all serious conversations about life. Mummy loves me very much.

Daddy is called Mike and he is important. He is a headmaster of a junior school. He is tallish and thinnish with fair hair and he is quite quiet and very nice to everybody which makes Mummy cross sometimes. He usually goes on Mark's side when Mummy has a big go at him. He loves me very much too. The best friend of our family is called Dip. I really love it when she is here. We all do. She makes us bright and we try more. She loves me too, but her eyes go softest when she looks at Mark.

This is a story about what happened just before Christmas when I was eight. We were all just sitting down to have lunch one Saturday, Dip as well, when Daddy came in with a letter in his hand.

"Look," he said, "here's a letter from Uncle Roger and Auntie Susan in Crawley."

Mark put his face nearly in his lunch and made a groaning sound.

Jack said, "Another report from the High Priest and Priestess?"

Mummy said, "Oh no, not more news of the sainted Emily."

The sainted Emily is my cousin who is just a bit younger than me. Uncle Roger and Auntie Susan are her parents and they are always going on about how good Emily is at everything and what a fantastic little sweetheart she is. Daddy just sighs about it, but Mummy gets all sarcastic and Mark does things like pretending to be sick – not in front of them I don't mean.

"What do they say?" asked Dip.

"Roger wants us to do him a favour," said Daddy. "Actually, he really wants Felicity to do him a favour."

Everybody looked at me. I tried to look like someone who doesn't mind doing favours for cousins they don't like.

Daddy said, "Uncle Roger wants to buy Emily a bike for Christmas, but he wants it to be a surprise. He says that since Emily and Felicity are roughly the same height and weight, would Felicity mind trying some bikes out in the local shops to see which ones

would be the right size? Then he'll come down just before Christmas and buy one of them and take it back with him for Emily."

I went all cold in my tummy. I wanted a brand new bicycle more
than anything else in the world and now the sainted Emily was
going to have one and I wasn't. My mouth was making little twitchy
movements and I could feel a big tear in each of my eyes, just prick-
ing my eyelids, but I managed to press my lips together and not let
the tears out.

"Happy to do that for Uncle Roger and Emily?" asked Daddy.

I made my head nod and I even managed to do a sort of twisty
smile.

"Can Dip take me?"

"Good heavens, yes," said Mummy, "I'm far too busy to shop for
Emily – if you don't mind, that is, Dip?"

Dip and me went off in her little yellow car and we spent all
Saturday afternoon in the three bike shops in the town. It was more
horrible than herrings. I kept forgetting that it wasn't me getting a
bike for Christmas so I would get all excited when I sat on a really
nice one, then suddenly remember that it was Emily whose sainted
little bottom would be sitting on the saddle on Christmas morning.
I did love some of those bikes so very much, especially a purple one
with silver rings on the straight metal bits. I hoped they wouldn't get
that one for Emily. Dip had a notebook to write down what she
called "the Results of our Research" and it was quite full by the time
we got home for tea.

"Well done!" said Daddy when he heard all about it. "You're a
good girl."

He gave me a sweet. A sweet!

I tried not to think about Emily's bike any more. On Christmas Eve I asked Daddy if Uncle Roger had been down to get it, and he said yes it was all sorted out thanks to me. Before I fell asleep I was excited because it was so nearly Christmas, but my mind couldn't stop thinking how Emily would feel tomorrow when she found her new bike leaning against the wall in the hall of her house.

When I got up before anyone else in the morning and went downstairs I found out exactly how she would have been feeling, because the purple bike with the silver rings was standing against the wall in our hall with a green ribbon and a label with my name on it tied round the thing you put your leg over. When I put my hands on the handlebars of my new bike I nearly cried again. Then I heard a noise and turned round and saw Mummy and Daddy standing at the bottom of the stairs looking at me and smiling.

Daddy said, "Sorry, darling, it was the only way I could think of to find out which bikes you liked best and which ones were the right size and still keep it a surprise. Dip helped. She knew all about it too. I'm afraid I made up the letter from Uncle Roger and Auntie Susan. I hope you don't mind. . . ."

I gave them both a Christmas hug, then I ran up the stairs as fast as I could to jump on Jack and Mark until they were awake enough to come and see what I'd got for Christmas.

Higher than the Angels
by Bridget Plass

"Well, we've sorted out our shepherds and kings and our innkeeper and our Mary and Joseph so now all we have to do ..."

Jess held her breath. She pressed her hands flat against her little round, churning tummy and stared stiffly ahead.

"... is to choose our angels. Four from this class and four from Mr Robinson's class. And this year, as Mary is to be played by Jenny Page from Mr Robertson's class, we are choosing our Angel Gabriel from this class."

Mrs Turner smiled round at her class of seven-year-olds. There were sixteen little girls in her class, and she knew almost all of them

75

were hoping against hope that they would be chosen. Gabriel was, after all, the only angel who spoke. She glanced down at her list and then up once more to smile at the children again. Jess tried to smile back. Tried to make it look as if it didn't matter. Tried desperately not to mind either way. After all, it didn't really matter, did it?

Oh, but it did! Of course it did. It mattered so very, very much. When you have two big sisters, both of whom are blonde and tall and pretty, and both of whom had played the Angel Gabriel when they were top infants, it *did* matter. Jess remembered her mother kneeling beside her biggest sister Beth and sewing gold tinsel round the hem of her shiny white dress. She herself must have been very little, of course. Beth had left Petworth Primary school last year and gone to the big school the other side of town, so when she was seven Jess must have only been three. Three years old, but she remembered her sister standing there in her shiny dress with gold wings and gold tinsel round her hair and thought she looked just like a beautiful princess. Then there was Anna who was just two years older than Jess. She had looked nice too, and Mummy had turned the dress up a little bit as Anna had not been quite so tall as Beth. Jess didn't remember feeling quite the same way about Anna, because actually Anna was rather bigheaded about being chosen, and Jess had got a bit fed up hearing about it as she lay each night in the bunk bed below Anna's. But she remembered thinking, *Next time it will be my turn, and I will be the pretty one and Anna will have to listen to me going on about it, and I'll go on and on and on about it even more than her, so there!*

Now that the moment had come Jess suddenly knew that she had been silly to assume that it would be her turn. Fifteen other girls in her class. Fifteen. She forced herself to think about them one by one, and suddenly, with horror, she knew exactly who was going to be Gabriel. It wasn't her. She glanced round. Sitting two tables behind her, Lauren, one of her best friends, twiddled her long silky fair hair with her little skinny fingers and smiled hopefully at her teacher. She was so pretty. So like Beth and Anna to look at and so not like Jess. Jess was little and round and had short amazingly curly brown hair, which her mummy said she had inherited from her Granddad. Granddad, who always called his three granddaughters his "Andy's angels" because their dad was called Andy, she supposed.

"Lauren dear, would you like to come here? Lauren, I would like you to be our Angel Gabriel this year. I am sure you will do a very good job."

Jess forced herself to clap with the others. She jolly well wouldn't mind. She could still go on and on at Anna even if she was only one of the ordinary angels with silver wings and silver tinsel.

But Jess didn't get to be one of the other angels either. Debby and Clare and Tania and Charlotte got to be the other angels, with silver tinsel and silver wings, and Jess got to be a carol singer. That's it. A person who wore a silly woollen hat and a scarf and who stood at the edge of the stage with all the rest of the choir and sang carols and didn't have anything to say at all, and that's not something you can go on and on about to your bighead big sister who is in the bunk above yours at night.

There was just one thing that happened before the day of Petworth Primary's infant nativity play that made Jess's humiliation bearable. The play was to take place on Thursday in the main hall, and on Tuesday everyone had to go to the hall for a practise, and it was then that the thing happened which made it all a bit better.

Every year the play was the same. The first scene was the Angel
Gabriel coming to see Mary, and the next scene was Mary and Joseph
going to Bethlehem and trying to find a room. Then it was the
innkeeper telling them he had a stable, and the next scene was when
Jesus was born. Then there were the shepherds keeping watch in their
fields by night, and the last scene was them coming to the stable and
the kings coming as well. It was the bit when the baby was going to be
born that the thing happened. Every year one of the boys in the choir
would carry the manger with the baby in it onto the stage and put it
down carefully in the middle just after the innkeeper showed Mary
and Joseph into the stable and just before the narrator said, "and the
time came for her to be delivered …"

This year, however, Mrs Turner decided that as there were more
boys than girls in the play and more girls than boys in her class it
would be a good idea to have a girl bring the crib and the baby Jesus
onto the stage. And the girl they had chosen was …

"Jess, we would like you to do it because you are a very sensible
girl and I know you will do it well."

What a lovely smile Mrs Turner had, and Jess, sitting cross-legged
on the floor with the rest of the cast, vowed she would try to do it
really, really well. What's more she would keep it a secret, and when
Anna came with her class to see the play, she would be amazed to see
Jess step out from the choir and go off stage to reappear with the
manger. The first ever girl at Petworth Primary school to do it.

And now at last it was Thursday afternoon, and out in the hall
were all the juniors sitting cross-legged in front of the stage, and
behind them lots and lots of mums and grans and babies and a few
dads, and there was a buzzy noise of them talking to each other. All
the children in the choir were standing in a line waiting to go onto

the stage. There was hardly any room at the side. At one point not everyone had been able to squash in there but Mr Robertson had said he would fix it, and after he had done something to fix it somehow they had just about managed to squeeze in.

Mrs Turner, standing with Mary and Gabriel, kept smiling at them all from the other side of the stage and putting her finger to her lips to remind them they mustn't make any noise at all, not even when Terry stepped on Louise's foot.

The choir went on first looking like carol singers and sang the first song, then Mary came onto the stage and sat on a little stool and the play had begun. It went really, really well. Apart from Joseph forgetting what he was supposed to say to the innkeeper, everyone did it just right. Then the choir was standing up to sing "Away in a Manger," and it was Jess's time to go off to her side of the stage and pick up the manger and bring it on. She went off stage and bent down to pick it up but something was wrong. It wasn't there. It had been there. Jess had seen it when she had first walked onto the side of the stage. Mr Robertson must have moved it so that they could all squash into the little space and forgotten to put it back. Where was it? Jess peeped through the curtain and saw it had been put down by the side of the piano. What was she going to do? She wanted to burst into tears, but she remembered that Mrs Turner had chosen her because she was a sensible girl, and she couldn't let her down. Parting the curtain she sat on the edge of the stage and quietly slid down onto the floor. The choir had just about got to the beginning of the last verse so there was no time to be lost. She couldn't lift the crib onto the stage, it was too heavy and the stage was too high. There was only one thing to do. Picking it up firmly Jess walked right down the side of the hall, along the back, and then, to the astonishment of Mary and Joseph, walked up the centre aisle and up the steps onto the stage. It wasn't easy. There were lots of feet sticking out, and an umbrella and a baby's buggy, but somehow she managed it, and at last, breathlessly, she arrived, deposited the crib in front of Mary, and rejoined the choir.

She had done it. Looking up she noticed Anna staring at her with horror and disgust. Oh no! Anna must have thought that she had got it wrong. Or worse, that she had just decided to show off. And what would Mrs Turner think? Would she be really, really cross? The last two scenes passed with Jess unable to take any of it in and at last it was over and the audience was clapping and everyone stood up and bowed and then sat down for the headmaster to come onto the stage just as he did every year.

"Thank you, everyone. As usual a splendid retelling of the Christmas story, but I must say it was a special surprise to me this year to have the story told a little bit differently. The bringing of the crib through the audience by one of the carol singers was a wonderful reminder to us that he came for all of us, not just to those born two thousand years ago, but to those of us who are alive today. Also the way Jess had to negotiate with dignity the difficulties in front of her reminds us of the difficult path Jesus chose to take in leaving his heavenly home to come and be with us. So, thank you, children, and thank you, Mrs Turner and Mr Robertson, for a lovely and thought-provoking afternoon."

"And the best bit," declared Jess as she retold her story for the fifth time to Anna that night, "was when Mrs Turner gave me a little hug and said she knew she could count on me and that they might keep it in and have a member of the choir carry the crib through the crowd next year. Just think, next year there may be a girl sitting in class hoping she will get to walk right round the hall with the crib and . . ."

"Jess, you did all right today, but I've just got one thing to say to you."

"Yes?"

"Stop going on and on and on and on and shut up and go to sleep!"

Little Tom's Letter to the Post Office

Little Tom was not looking forward to Christmas. It had been a very difficult year for every single member of his family, and there were no signs at all of things improving in the near future.

As Christmas got nearer and nearer all the other children in Tom's class at school started to talk about the fun and games they were going to have, the good food they were planning to eat, and the presents they were hoping to give and receive. Tom tried to join in, but it just made him feel sad. In the end he made up reasons for drifting off to the other end of the playground, or out to the toilets if it was cold and rainy and the class had to play or eat their lunch indoors. He tried not to think about Christmas at all because it was so upsetting.

One weekend, as he sat at home in his bedroom feeling hungry because there wasn't much money for food, and cold because the heating had been turned off after his mother and father found themselves unable to pay the electricity bill, he decided to write to Father Christmas, explaining the problems his family were facing and asking for a little help. This is what he said in his letter:

Dear Father Christmas,

I do not know if you will ever get this letter but thank you for reading it if you do. Do not worry if you do not. I am writing to tell you that things are very bad at our house. My daddy has been very ill and has lost all his money because his best friend who he worked with ran off to a place called South America taking all Daddy's money with him. Daddy is too poorly to work and so he cannot pay for Christmas. Mummy would go out to work but she had an accident tripping over Daddy when he was in despair on the stairs and has been told she must lie down and not move for six weeks. My brother had a good job but two weeks ago he was made something called redundant and he owes lots of money that he cannot go on paying off now because there is no money coming in and he has to hide. Our dog is sick and needs treatment but we cannot afford the vet's bills, and there is a hole in our roof with rain forecast.

Please could you send us a hundred pounds so that we can at least have a nice Christmas?

Love,
Tommy

When Tommy's letter arrived at the Post Office, addressed to "Father Christmas, Greenland," one of the men who worked in the sorting office opened it up and showed a group of his friends what Tommy had written.

"Look chaps," he said, "this little lad needs a bit of help, so why don't we have a collection round the office and send him whatever we get? He's put his address on the letter so we'll just send him the money as if it's come from Father Christmas. What do you say?"

Everyone thought it was a great idea. By that evening they had managed to collect eighty pounds to send to Tommy. The next morning one of them put it through his door with a little note saying "Here you are, Tommy. Love, Father Christmas."

Two days later another envelope addressed to Father Christmas, Greenland, arrived at the Post Office. The postmen opened it eagerly, keen to read little Tom's letter of thanks. This is what they read:

Dear Father Christmas,

Thank you ever so much for the money. I only got eighty pounds of it, but then, you know what those thieving beggars at the Post Office are like. . . .

A Special Day
by Bridget Plass

Moving calmly through the frenzied shoppers clogging the aisles of her local supermarket, Miranda felt a certain sense of calm superiority. Not for her an overflowing trolley packed with huge joints of meat, enough vegetables and bread to feed an army, tubs of ice-cream, tins of fruit, crackers, cakes, and chocolates indicating hours of work in the kitchen for the woman trying to manoeuver it. This year she was to have none of that. This year was to be different. A Christmas of indulgence. A Christmas just for her. A special day.

Taking her place in the Ten Items or Less queue, she glanced down at the contents of her basket and allowed herself a small smile.

A bottle of excellent red wine, a thick fillet steak, frozen prawns, a prepack of luxury vegetables, an individual Christmas pudding, some outrageously expensive fresh strawberries, a small tub of clotted cream, and a tiny box of luxury Belgian chocolates nestled next to her favourite romantic comedy video and a bottle of exclusive bath essence. On impulse she added an expensive glossy magazine from the rack next to the till and laughingly begged the young shop assistant to let her off having eleven instead of ten purchases.

"Just this once. After all it is Christmas!" smiled the girl as she handed Miranda her change. "Have a happy one."

A happy Christmas. Was that what it was going to be? For a split second the pleasure with which she had chosen the items to enhance her day threatened to fade, but immediately she took control. Of course it would be happy. She had decided. A luxury, indulgent day just for her. And anyway it had to be much better than last year's, which had been the worst Christmas in her entire life.

Loading the car boot with her purchases, she noticed a group of children being organised into rows in the forecourt of the supermarket, presumably about to sing carols to the exhausted shoppers on this Christmas Eve. As she joined the queue of cars to drive at snail's pace out of the car park her prediction came true. The enthusiastic child voices singing "Silent Night" at top volume caused a sudden lurch of emotions that almost caused her to momentarily lose control of the wheel.

"How sweet," she muttered firmly to herself as she turned her car radio on at full volume. "Just the right touch. The ideal start to some people's Christmas. All that stuff. Now home and let the fun begin."

Soaking in her bath, the swirls of lavender-scented mist made her feel relaxed and rather special. Pampered. Expensive. She spent the rest of the evening by the fire watching her video and sipping sherry and feeling pleasantly sleepy. Now all she needed was a good night's sleep in order to enjoy the next day to the full. Picking up her new magazine, she padded upstairs to bed. The house was incredibly quiet. Serene. She would sleep like a log.

By four in the morning she had to admit she had been wrong. Sitting up in bed and turning her sidelight on for the umpteenth time, she acknowledged defeat. She hadn't slept. Her plan hadn't worked. The relaxing lavender essential oil bath essence had not fulfilled its promise. The glossy magazine had been read from cover to cover but hadn't proved the successful distraction she had planned. The sherry that had made her feel so drowsy the evening before hadn't knocked her out for the night. Her pillows had been turned and plumped a hundred times. She had even gone downstairs to the kitchen at about two in the morning to make a cup of tea. But the luxurious sleep she had anticipated had totally evaded her and she felt cross, tired, and incredibly alone.

The sudden ringing of her telephone caused her to hurtle down the stairs, her heart thumping against her ribs so strongly that she could hardly speak as she lifted the receiver. Something must be terribly wrong for the phone to go at this ridiculous hour of the night.

"Is that you?"

Words didn't come.

"Mummy," the voice was a whisper, "is that you?"

"Sam, darling, of course it's me. What's wrong?"

"Nothing's wrong, Mummy. I just thought you'd like to know that you were right, Mummy. Father Christmas did know that I would be at Daddy's new house this year and not at home with you. He's been,

Mummy. Father Christmas has been, and I've felt my pillow case and, Mummy . . ."

"Yes, darling."

"Mummy, I think . . . I *think* he's given me Woody from *Toy Story*. We saw him in the shop. Do you remember, Mummy? The one with the hat that comes off. Do you remember?"

"Of course I remember, Sam."

"Well, I'd better go and get back into bed now. Daddy and Sally are asleep. I just thought you'd be really pleased to know. . . . Well, that's what I thought. . . ."

She could hear the faint bewilderment creeping into his whispering voice.

"Oh Sam. Of course I'm pleased, darling. Of course I am. It's just – I'm not surprised. After all we did sit down and write a letter to Father Christmas telling him that you would be at Daddy's this year, didn't we, and we did put the address didn't we? Ring me again tomorrow morning, won't you, and tell me if he did bring you a Woody."

"I will – but, Mummy, it may be a bit late."

Why? Why would it be late? What magnificent treat had her ex-husband and his new lady planned for her son on his first Christmas away from his mother, that would prevent her son from phoning her until "a bit late". The familiar debilitating combination of anger and hurt that had dogged her life for the last two years filled her whole being, but she struggled to control her voice as she asked, "Oh? Why is that, Sam?"

"Because I think Daddy's taking me to the family service at church. Just him and me. Well, that's what I think. I heard him and Sally talking last night, and he said to her that he wanted to take me because that's what you would like. Mummy? Mummy, are you still there? Mummy, you're not upset are you? You're not goin' to cry are you? It's a *nice* thing he said, isn't it?"

"Yes, Sam. It's a very, very nice thing he said. Sam . . . ?"

"Yes, Mummy?"

"Have a lovely Christmas, and it doesn't matter one little bit if you ring a bit late. I've just decided I might go to church myself anyway. I'll think of you and you think of me, and we'll both think of Jesus being born. Okay? And Sam – can you do a special thing for me? Can you tell Daddy and Sally I said 'Happy Christmas'. You won't forget, will you?"

"No, I won't, and yes, I will – tell them, I mean. Mummy, you know I love you lots and lots, don't you?"

"Sam, go to bed, you nutcase. Of course I do."

"Have a Happy Christmas, Mummy."

"I will, Sam. Do you know I really think I might."

"Night night, Mummy. Or" – a little giggle – "morning, morning!"

"Morning morning, Sam and – God bless."

Coping with Christmas, Not Religious But Nice

Adrian, Anne, and their irreverent son, Gerald, first saw the light in the mid-eighties in *The Sacred Diary of Adrian Plass – aged 37 3/4*. The main protagonist in this fictional account is Adrian, a good-hearted twit who records his adventures without realising how much of himself he is actually revealing. I suppose there is quite a lot of me in this character, but I only gave him my name because the *Adrian Mole* diary books were very popular at the time, and I never realised how many people would eventually read the book and its successors. The other main characters are purely fictitious. Adrian's wife, Anne, is wise, kind, and long-suffering. Their son, Gerald, is a likeable young man who finds much Christian behaviour far too funny to take seriously.

People often ask me where the Diary characters came from. Was there ever really a Leonard Thynn? What about the dreadful Flushpools, the frightening Cooks, the wise Edwin, and the seductive Gloria Marsh? Are they all based on real people? Well, the only honest answer to that question is that the best and worst of these people come from me, from you, from the man next door, and from all the other people who have ever tried to follow Jesus, and a few of those who haven't. God bless us all, everyone, I say.

Sunday December 15th

Another commercial Christmas! I shall send only ten cards this year. What is Christmas about, after all?

Our church is getting like an auction room. One blink and you get ministered to. Sit still and keep your eyes shining – that's my motto. This morning was Edwin Burlesford's fault. Forty-five minutes on "sin"! A record nine-fruit-gum talk. Halfway through, I was checking supplies when Edwin suddenly shouted "LUST!" and made me drop the packet under my chair. Put my head down between my knees to locate it, then couldn't get up because Doreen Cook pressed her hands down on the back of my head. She prayed that "our despairing brother would move from darkness to light". I was all for that – I couldn't see a thing. When she let me get up she had one of those roguish Christian smiles on her face. Came very close to really giving her something to forgive me for. Everyone thinks I've got a big lust problem now. At coffee time they all smiled reassuringly at me. Leonard Thynn hugged me. I signed Edwin's carol-singing list for next Saturday to show that I'm not all bad. Gerald's coming too.

Monday December 16th

My son, Gerald, says James Bond is on next Saturday evening. Pity it clashes. Still, carol-singing is the Lord's work.

Absent-mindedly bought a box of fifty Christmas cards. Never mind – that's enough for five years.

Tuesday December 17th

Dreamt last night that I *was* James Bond.

Wednesday December 18th

Is carol-singing scriptural? Rang Doreen Cook's husband, Richard, who thinks Christmas trees are wrong. No luck – apparently it's okay.

Bought another fifty cards.

Thursday December 19th

Could it be that God's trying to say I *should* watch James Bond? Opened my Bible at random and put my finger on the page. It said,

"The dogs licked up the blood."

Went to bed. I don't understand God sometimes. . . .

Friday December 20th

Laid a "fleece". If a midget in a Japanese admiral's uniform came to the door at 9.04 precisely, I would know that God wanted me to sing carols.

9.05: A miracle! No one came. That's that then. Leonard Thynn came at 10.30 selling charity cards. Bought fifty.

Saturday December 21st

What an evening!

7.30: Film started. Surprised to find Gerald settling down to watch. "What about carol-singing?" I said. "Oh, no," he replied, "I rang old Edwin on Monday and told him there was a good film on, so I wouldn't be going."

Why don't I do things like that?

8.45: Edwin at the door, concerned as I hadn't gone carol-singing. Lost my nerve and told him I was still fretting over my lust problem.

11.00: Edwin left after counselling me for two-and-a-quarter hours. Missed the end of the film. As he left, Edwin said, "I'm off home to watch that Bond film. The wife's videoed it."

Gerald said it was the best ending to a film he'd ever seen. He grinned in a rather unchristian manner when he said this. He's a good lad though. Patted my head and said he thought God liked me despite everything.

Next year I am not sending *any* Christmas cards

. . . Despite what???

Had some news today that would be really depressing if we weren't Christians. Anne's Uncle Ralph, who is the most vulgar man I have ever met, will have to spend Christmas with us. Wouldn't be so bad, only we've already got my Great Aunt Marjorie staying from tomorrow. *She* condemns wine-gums for their "intoxicant potential"! Gerald rubbed his hands when he heard the news.

Oh, dear . . .

Monday December 23rd

Met Gerald in the hall when I got back from work. He said, "The Titanic has docked."

Found Aunt Marjorie looking through the TV magazines in the sitting room. After we had exchanged the customary kiss in which not even the tiniest part of my face touches the tiniest part of hers, she said, "I am encircling with black ink those programmes that are unsuitable and which we shall *not* be watching during the Christmas period!"

Gerald poked his head round the door, and said, "There's a man at the door with a deliverance ministry."

Turned out to be the postman doing a late round. A parcel and two cards. Counted the cards we've received so far after everybody had gone to bed tonight. Not as many as last year. Naturally, I forgive all those who've forgotten us, but you'd think they could make a bit more effort. After all, that's what Christmas is all about, isn't it?

Uncle Ralph arrives tomorrow.

What on earth will Marjorie make of him?

Gerald says he makes Bernard Manning look like the Archbishop of Canterbury.

Tuesday December 24th

How is it possible for someone like Anne to have an uncle like Ralph? He arrived just after lunch, a short, very fat man, on a tiny motor scooter. Life is just one big whoopee cushion to Uncle Ralph.

Disastrous first encounter with Great Aunt Marjorie. Kissed her full on the lips, and said, "No one told me there was going to be some spare talent on the menu this Christmas. Stick around Marjy-girl. You could be right up little Ralphy's street!"

Aunt Marjorie turned puce and has refused to look at him, let alone talk to him all evening, even when he flicked through the Radio Times and said, "Heh! Good biz! Someone's gone through and marked off all the best progs!"

Anne and I arranged all the presents under the Christmas tree tonight. The ones from Uncle Ralph are all shaped like bottles.

Asked Anne what she thinks God loves about Uncle Ralph. She said, "His niece." Kissed.

Wednesday December 25th

Christmas Day!

Aunt Marjorie went off to a "proper church" this morning.

Ralph not up by the time Gerald and Anne and I left for the Christmas service.

Enjoyed it all very much except for a point halfway through the prayer-time, when George Farmer, who was sitting behind me, stood up and began to swing his fist from side to side as he prayed fervently for goodwill among God's people.

Suddenly felt a heavy blow on the side of my head and slumped forward, momentarily stunned. Shook my head to clear it and realised to my amazement that Farmer was still ranting on as if nothing had happened!

Didn't feel much goodwill.

I said to him afterwards, "I forgive you for punching me in the head, George."

He said, "Did I really do that?"

Gerald said, "Yes you did. It was on your twenty-fifth 'just' – I was counting."

Went home.

Spent the rest of the day rugby-tackling Uncle Ralph's jokes before they could cross the line. Became more and more difficult as he drank more and more whisky.

After tea, he went up to his room to get something "really good" for a game he knew.

Came back with a rubber monkey attached to a long length of elastic and told Great Aunt Marjorie she should stuff the monkey down her dress, pull it out at the bottom, and pass it to him so that he could put it down his trousers, then pass it to Anne.

Thought for a moment she was going to faint.

She retired to bed early, leaving the bottle of gin that Ralph gave her this morning, unopened in the wastepaper basket near the foot of the stairs.

Gerald, who seems to have enjoyed the day enormously, asked Ralph if he knew any more "good games".

Ralph said the best game he knew was one where you sit in a circle and each person drinks a bottle of whisky, then one person goes out of the room, and the others have to guess who it was.

How can you run a Christian household with people like Uncle Ralph around?!

I could be a really good Christian if other people didn't mess it up all the time.

I've noticed this before.

Mentioned it to Anne in bed tonight.

She said, "Well, I promise you, darling, that Gerald and I will try really hard not to stand in the way of your saintliness."

Just a hint of satire there, I fancy.

Thursday December 26th

Richard Cook turned up this morning to invite us to the Fellowship New Year's Eve party.

Talked in the kitchen.

Dreaded Uncle Ralph appearing suddenly and saying something really awful.

Afraid I wasn't altogether honest.

I said "Anne's Uncle Ralph is staying with us this Christmas, Richard. He's not a Christian, and he can be – well – let's say, difficult, but I honestly think part of our witness has to be showing a spirit of tolerance and perhaps even giving the impression sometimes that we enjoy or laugh at things that might be – well – not quite on."

Said this because I hadn't been able to help laughing at one or two of Ralph's dirty jokes, and knowing him, he was quite likely to say to Richard, "Here's a good one! Adrian nearly wet himself when he heard this one!"

As for witness, it never crossed my mind in connection with Uncle Ralph. Not the Christian type, I suppose.

Amazed when we took our coffee into the sitting room to find that a miracle seemed to have happened. Ralph shook hands quietly and politely with Richard, and insisted on leading him to the most comfortable chair, saying, "It's a real pleasure to meet one of Adrian's friends. Do sit down."

As Richard put his weight on the chair, a most awful noise came from underneath him. Shot to his feet again, and Uncle Ralph lifted up the cushion to reveal a deflated rubber bladder with the words "A REAL BRONX CHEER" printed on the side. Ralph was in hysterics of course.

Richard, obviously taking to heart what I'd said in the kitchen, started to cackle in his high-pitched artificial sort of way and said, "Oh, what a good joke against me! I don't disapprove of it. Oh, no! I think it's very funny. Ha, ha!"

Very ashamed.

Rang Richard later and confessed I'd not been very truthful.

Give old Richard his due, whether it's thick skin or love I'm not sure, but he doesn't bear grudges.

Told Anne and Gerald what had happened when they came in.

Anne, who'd been out on a disapproval tour of the area with Aunt Marjorie, was rather short with me.

Gerald made me tell him what had happened three times over. Could still hear him laughing hours later when we were all in bed.

Thank goodness Marjorie and Ralph are leaving tomorrow.

We've all had enough really.

Tuesday December 31st

To the Cooks' at 9.00 P.M. for the church's New Year's Eve party. Earlier on I had said, "We'll take quiche, shall we?"

Anne said, "Cake would probably be better."

Gently reminded Anne that Scripture tells us the man is the head of the woman. We took quiche.

Everyone took quiche! No sandwiches, no cake, no puddings, just acres of – quiche.

Anne said, "What now, oh Lord and Master?"

Gerald said the Lord's Prayer should change to "Give us this day our daily quiche, because that's all Christians ever eat."

Richard Cook was standing nearby and overheard. He said it was mocking the Word, and did Gerald really have assurance?

Gerald foolishly replied, "Yes, I'm with the Woolwich."

Richard stormed off towards the raspberryade. I wish Gerald wouldn't do it.

Left after an hour or two of loud embarrassing games organised by George Farmer.

In the garden on the way out, we found Leonard Thynn having a theological debate with a large garden gnome and drinking something from a Tizer bottle. Took him home, Gerald insisting on staying to see him in and put him to bed. Typical Gerald. Not religious—but nice.

Christmas at St. Yorick's

The pieces in the following section all come from *A Year at St. Yorick's*, a book that purports to be twelve months of collected magazines from the Parish of Gently Down, a small village somewhere in England. Edited by Henry Pitcher with the assistance of the vicar's secretary, Miss Fitt, the publication does its best to rise above the normal expectations of an Anglican church magazine. However, success in this aspiration is limited. Some things never seem to change. Misprints, for instance . . .

Report on Parish Carol Singing Expedition
by George Pain

I dunno. I'm no good at this. Henry made me do it. Well, we went, didn't we? What can I say? I went. Lots of people went. It was dark. Thank God! We only went to people over near where Dave Billings lives, who, for reasons that are beyond me, had lied through their teeth about being really keen on having people singing dead badly outside their houses just as Eastenders started.

Well, as usual we lurched along in a body behind Dave Billings from lamppost to lamppost like a pack of incontinent dogs. As far as I can remember there were some instruments being played by two or three musically independent spirits, one blowy thing, two scrapey things, and an infernal, blasted squeezy thing that needed to be strangled or have something evil cast out of it. Sounded more like a punishment squad sent to carry sentence out on erring church members, than a group supposed to be bringing pleasure to the local populace. Pretended to the kids that we were doing them a favour by letting them collect money from the doors, instead of admitting we were all chicken about the prospect of getting a load of abuse from the odd Marxist music lover.

Got lost towards the end when Dave Billings, describing himself jovially as "The Local Lad", said he knew a good short cut. Ended up all slipping down this nightmarish, grassy bank in the pitch dark into some obscure railway cutting. Everyone a bit frightened and hysterical until the Local Lad calmed everybody by explaining that it was an old branch line that hadn't been used for years. General laughter and cries of relief abruptly curtailed by the arrival of a blasted train! All escaped by scrambling up the bank in a panic – women, children, and little Georgy Pain first. The player of the infernal squeezy blasted thing was last up, unfortunately still clutching his weapon. Very tempted to give him a sharp shove with the sole of my boot just as he got to the top of the slope.

Almost back at Local Lad Dave's house when that weird old Italian bloke stopped under a lamppost, burst into tears, and began singing some plaintive song in his own language in a very high voice. Not much remaining on the procreational side there, if you ask me. Hilary Tuttsonson, knowing that the lease on his flat's about to run out, called it a very moving moment. I didn't think it was, but then I don't do Bed and Breakfast with reductions for church members. The bloke who lived in the house he was singing outside didn't think it was very moving either. Opened his front door and called out in a heavy Australian accent like a twanging elastic band that he was going to set his two Tasmanian devils on us if we didn't stuff a sock in Caruso's gob and clear off. Nobody really thought he had any Tasmanian devils, but we didn't half shift, including Garibaldi, or whatever he's called, who manfully conquered his grief and galloped away like a whippet with an itchy bottom. He'd obviously not reached such a point of sobbing sadness that he didn't mind having bits of himself chewed off by little Antipodean growling things.

Arrived at Dave's house at last. Good old Dave and Mrs Dave had got it all together for once and laid on mulled wine and mince pies and other festive bits and pieces. Must have cost more than we collected all evening. Still, good laugh really. Nobody got blotto. One or two tried hard. Garibaldi cheered up. Preferred him when he was miserable, I think. Nice bunch of people, I suppose, most of them. Be good and right to arrange a lynch-mob for the bloke with the haunted, squeezy, ear-torturing blasted thing. Next Christmas maybe?

A Letter from the Vicar

Dearly Beloved,

My wife, Elspeth, and I would like to wish a very happy and prosperous new year to all in the parish, although such wishes for your prosperity should not necessarily be interpreted as referring to the acquisition of material gains, innocent though such acquisition may be when fuelled by the appropriate motivation, but to the acquisition of that spiritual treasure which Our Lord so frequently advised his listeners to store up in heaven, nor is my reference to happiness intended to exclude

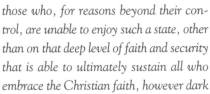

those who, for reasons beyond their control, are unable to enjoy such a state, other than on that deep level of faith and security that is able to ultimately sustain all who embrace the Christian faith, however dark

their circumstances may appear to become, and, of course, these wishes are extended to all outside the parish as well as to those in it, since, as Christians, it is our duty to extend love to the entire world and not just those close to us, although that is, naturally, bound to be in a theoretical sense, as we are not actually able to personally know the entire population of the world, which is perhaps just as well, as the yearly bill for Christmas cards would be prohibitive, although I make that point only as a humorous aside, a residue perhaps of that Yuletide spirit which has been at the centre of our lives so very recently.

What is it, dear friends, that is special about this time of year? I wonder if you have noticed. Well, here is a clue. Exactly the same thing could be said of my underpants and my socks – at least, those underpants and socks that Elspeth presented me with in such an attractively exciting

package at six A.M. on the morning of Christmas Day. Yes, you are absolutely correct – they were new! My underpants and socks, still in their Cellophane wrappers, are wonderfully new, and so, in a very real sense, is the year that is about to begin even as I write.

What does being new really mean?

Well, my attempts (under considerable pressure from my wife and the new editor of the magazine) to make this monthly letter more jovial in tone are new. A baby is new. The Rolling Stones, however unacceptable they may be to many of us, are new. Our blessedly lively young curate, Curtis, is new. Channel Four on the television service is new. All of these things share a quality of newness, do they not, friends? A freshness, an aura of beginningness, a sense of not being old, an attribute of commencement, a common aspect of recent appearance, a feeling of not having been here before. And all can be sadly misused. To both the year that is about to begin and to my underwear, God has given a specific purpose. Bearing in mind that the secular world is always watching, I shall feel it my duty to fill the next twelve months with just as much care as I fill socks and my underpants.

How about you?

> From the desk of your vicar,
> Richard Harcourt-Smedley

P.S. Another new thing is the style of this magazine under its new editor, Henry Pitcher, who tells me that he is hoping to cultivate a new openness and frankness over the months to come. I would merely utter a word of caution to the effect that such revolutionary concepts as openness and frankness should be introduced very gradually to any Anglican community.

A Poem for Christmas
Talking Turkey
by Sarah Forrest

Gobble, gobble, turkey birds,
Gobble from the heart,
Gobble, gobble all you can,
Before the humans start.

A Christmas Household Hint
Sent in by Maude Dent

At Christmas-time empty milk bottles seem to breed, don't they? Well, how about this for an idea? On Christmas Day, perhaps at a point

when things seem to have temporarily gone a little flat, go quietly into the kitchen without telling anyone and collect together ten empty milk bottles. Stand them on the kitchen table and put each of your ten fingers and thumbs into a separate bottle. You will find it quite easy to keep the bottles in place after you lift your hands. Now, burst into the room in which most people are gathered, and, clinking the bottles together with your fingers and thumbs, shout out loudly, "Edward Bottlehands!" Things won't be flat after that! Why not let the kids have a go when you've finished?

Advertisement

How beautiful on the mountains are the feet of those who bring good news? The answer is – not very, if they haven't had those ugly corns treated. Christian chiropodist. Special Yuletide

reductions for those who want to make use of me the living leg
end. Ring 560278

Noticeboard

- This month's Ladies Circle meeting will be held on Thursday
  December 18th at 36, Butterwick Avenue. This will be a
  "Singalong-a-Satan" evening (he may even put in an appearance!), with mince-pies, sherry, and, just
  before our husbands take us home, the
  exchanging of small gits.

- The parish carol-singing expedition will
  set forth on Friday 19th of December at 6.30
  P.M. And let's have a few younger folk this
  year! Please gather outside the vicarage for
  the distribution of snogsheets. If you play
  an instrument bring it along. Vaughn Clar-
  idge will be in New Malden.

- The parish Carol Service will be held on Sunday December 21st
  at 6.30 P.M. in the church. A chance to relax for those who are
  itching to get away from the Christmas rash.

- At 5.30 P.M. on Wednesday 24th December (Christmas Eve) we
  shall be holding our Christingle service, in the course of which
  children are given an orange and a candle in symbolic welcome
  of the baby Jesus, the light of the world, into our midst. Members
  of the Mother and Toddler group that meets regularly in the
  church hall are specially invited to attend this very moving service, but please keep very small children at the back, and note
  that the church and its servants and employees cannot be held
  responsible for damage or injury caused in any way whatsoever

by the flame of the said candles, or by any object or surface that that has been heated or ignited by that flame.

- A warm welcome to all!
- There will be a midnight service this year, but after our problems last time, it has been decided that any incidents of drunkenness will be dealt with most severely. The opening carol will be "God Help you Merry Gentlemen."
- Our Christmas Day service will be a Family Service, and will begin at 10.30 A.M. The vicar's wife will encourage children to come to the front and display the contents of their stockings to the congregation, just as she has been doing every year since she first came to the parish.
- A "Nearly-There New Year's Eve Party" will be held at the Jaw home, 25, Forwill Drive, from 8.00 P.M. until midnight. Admission by unsaved friend and any bottle or carton of soft-drink. Choruses will be sung.
- Single Anglican lady wishing to remain anonymous in case of embarrassing her employer at the vicarage, would like to respond to George Pain's very moving lines in the November magazine by saying that she has been chewing moss, and it works! She would be very happy to kiss him in any month of the year, and that includes the mistless ones in which he is clearly risible.

Children's Corner
Born-Again Toads

A lovely present for the daddy who's got everything
Contributed by Liz Turton

Don't throw away those old used drinks cartons this Christmas, children, or the straws that come with them. After only a very little easy cutting and sticking, you can enjoy making an extra present to give Daddy. His very own, road-flattened, inflatable, born-again toad!

Simply squeeze the carton flat, then cut out and stick a leg to each corner. Next, cut a head shape and stick it on one end. Mix some mud-coloured paint and carefully paint your toad with a line down the back, and eyes and a mouth on the head.

Leave to dry.

Now the fun can start!

After Daddy has unwrapped his present tell him to insert a straw into the hole in one end of his toad-carton and blow hard.

The flattened toad should come magically back to life as the carton is inflated!

HOURS OF FUN!

Christmas in America and England

You Say Tomato, which I wrote with the American Paul McCusker, tells the story of two rather troubled Christians: George Smith, who is English, and Bradley Miller, an American. After meeting at a conference in England, the two men agree to exchange letters across the Atlantic. In the course of this correspondence they discover that cultural differences are far less significant than the deeply important things they have in common.

27ᵗʰ December

Dear George,

Thank you for the letter and the terrific angel to put on the top of Mom's tree. It arrived Christmas Eve. Mom was deeply touched, though when I wanted to just stick the thing on the tree, she rebuked me and turned the placement of the angel into a formal-almost-religious experience, complete with the angel held high and a hymn being sung ("Angels We have Heard on High") as we marched to the tree and put it on top. When I teased Mom about "going liturgical," she just shrugged.

I took that opportunity to tell her what I told you about leaving my church in order to find something "more traditional". I braced myself for an argument. Instead, she said she understood completely. Good thing, since I had already made plans to go to the Christmas Eve service at an old, old Episcopal church (built in 1927). I was surprised to realize that the Episcopalians are American Anglicans. What a coincidence, huh? I was even more surprised when she asked to go with me. The church is cathedral-like and very reverent, and the Christmas Eve service was one of the most beautiful I've ever seen. It scratched the itch, George. I'll have to go back. Mom agreed.

Christmas Day was spent quietly enough – just the two of us and the obligatory calls from my half-brother and two half-sisters. They're scattered around the country and have families of their own. I also get the impression that they're avoiding Mom's illness. True to the American spirit, we avoid dealing with death at every turn.

Sorry about the Sears gift certificate (token?). I really thought they were an international chain. Tell me how much the Boots certificate was and I'll send you a check right away. Otherwise, plan to use the Sears certificate when you come to visit (hint, hint).

I talked to Mom about your renewed interest in the opposite sex. She noted that your preoccupation with Diane's sweater telegraphed your interest, whether you realized it or not. She mentioned a seed in winter or something like that.

Somehow it doesn't seem appropriate to ramble on about sex right after Christmas, but I will say that American Christians take it very seriously. After years of not discussing it or drilling into adolescent minds how horrible it is if you abuse it, we now have a smorgasbord of books proclaiming it as God-ordained and pleasurable and wonderful (in the context of marriage, of course), and even how to do it in a true spiritual way. Don't ask, I don't know. As a single man, I can't relate, and I find there are very few books for my situation (being single and staying pure, etc.) – at least none that I'm interested in reading. Illustrations would help.

Of course, being a single male at the age of twenty-eight is tantamount to proclaiming myself gay to all the world anyway. (A worthwhile discussion for our book, I think: What happens to singles in England? What do you think of homosexuality? – and don't blame me for asking because you brought up the whole sex subject.) I have an experience to tell you about, but not now.

I got a nice little note from Diane, by the way. She is convinced that Mom is going to be healed – if we have enough faith. I wonder how much faith will be a suitable bribe for God?

Brad

P.S. Happy New Year!

4th January

Dear Bradley,

I've been picturing the following scene: It's Christmas Eve in heaven. (I'm afraid they probably don't have a Sears department store in heaven either, Brad, but you'll just have to get by the best you can.) There's been some excitement in the Golden City lately because Bradley Miller of Colorado, America, has started to see a way forward for his faith. His route, carefully worked out by God and cleared of obstacles specially for him by an angelic road-gang, if he did but know it, runs through the traditional Church in general, and, in particular, an old, old Episcopal church (built in 1927) near his home.

God is so excited. He's had a very soft spot for this young American for many years, and now, at last, after a great deal of planning and organization, something of real spiritual significance is going to happen. On Christmas morning, the Father of all mankind is pacing the floor of heaven, awaiting angelic intelligence of Bradley Miller's response to the experience that has been designed to flood him with an awareness of the power and love of God in his life. At last the Miller angel, tired and haggard beyond his years, presents himself before his Master and kneels respectfully.

"Well?" demands God. "Don't just kneel there – tell me what he said! Did he speak in tongues at last? Did he break into hymns of praise? Did he dance in the Spirit? What did he say? Tell me!"

"He said – "

"Yes, what?"

"He said, 'It scratched the itch.'"

"I'm so glad he was pleased," says God, slightly miffed.

I'm glad you were pleased as well, Brad. As you must have gathered from what I wrote back in autumn, I tend to go in that sort of direction as well, but only because it's right for me. Everyone else can join the Ninth Day Amber-Bryanites for all I care. Goodness, how relieved everyone else must be.

I'm glad I didn't have to be there to watch your family taking obligatory steps. How dreary. You've never told me anything about your father. Dead? Alive? Goody? Baddy? Christian? Episcopalian?

We spent Christmas with my divorced sister, Jenny, and her three little girls, up in Bishop Auckland, near Durham. (If you come over next year, I must show you Durham – such a beautiful city.) We had a wonderful time for three very good reasons.

One, it's the first Christmas since Gemma's death that I haven't been locked into the business of clenching my pain with both fists and pretending I was all right for Cherry's sake. I actually felt happy!

Two, I was back with God – nearly made a complete idiot of myself on Christmas morning at church. I just couldn't stop the tears when I went up for communion. The Body of Christ, broken for me; the Blood of Christ, shed for me – staggering. Good job it was one of the more stolid Anglican churches. They were more likely to offer me hay-fever tablets than ministry.

Third, it was good to be with Jenny and the girls. Cherry had a wonderful time being all girly with her cousins. It was worth hacking through forests of underwear in the bathroom every morning and evening to see her so happy. It's the first time Jenny and I have properly supported each other since Gemma died. Jenny's husband, who provides excellent opportunities for the exercise of forgiveness, left her eighteen months ago, and she really has had to struggle. We got slightly tipsy together on Boxing Day evening. I hope God didn't mind too much. . . .

You asked me what happens to single people in England. Well, the short answer is that they tend to be marginalized by people from the church, not for malicious reasons, but just because people forget that, if you are on your own, you don't always have the confidence to inflict yourself on families. You need to be invited specifically to join people in their homes, rather than be told it's "all right to drop in any time". I feel awful when I think back to the way Gemma and I were with single people. We were so insensitive – but we didn't understand, you see? Besides all that, the Church as an institution is very much geared to family activity, and you can feel very uncared-for at times. I've tended to sulk about this in the past, but I think I'm going to make more of an effort to let people know how singles feel – then it'll be up to them.

As for the issue of homosexuality – well, I am gay, as you've probably already guessed. I'm not really gay. Sorry, Bradley. I only said that so you could find out how your perception of me changed at the moment when you thought I was homosexual. Oh, Brad, I find this such a difficult subject. Can't I chicken out?

"No, you can't."

Who said that?

"Me."

Oh, all right, then. If you drove me into a corner and threatened to play Scottish music to me until I came out with what I really thought, I'd have to say that I don't think homosexual behaviour is something that God is happy about, any more than he's happy about the way in which vast numbers of heterosexuals conduct themselves. But more importantly than any of that, I believe – I know – that it's no easier now to outguess God in individual situations than it was when Jesus was here in the flesh.

I've been told to love people and not judge them. I'd rather do that than home in on their sexuality. Oh biscuits! I don't know!

You had an experience? Oh, dear . . .

Ask Diane if she's willing to come and get her jumper if it turns out she's wrong about your mum being healed. That'll test her faith, if not yours.

Love to Mary from Cherry and me. The fire's all ready to light if she wants to come.

Love from George

Part Four

AND A CHILD SHALL LEAD THEM

Jesus says that we should become like little children. This statement has many layers of meaning, but when I remember my own children's eyes on Christmas morning when they were little, I begin to understand what he means.

Image of the Invisible God

Every now and then a familiar line of Scripture strikes me in a completely new way. Yes, you're right, I suppose if I gave more time to studying the Bible that would happen much more frequently, but never mind. We can only do something we call our best but probably isn't really. Anyway, the particular bit I have in mind at the moment is the fifteenth verse of Colossians where Paul says that Christ is the image of the invisible God. Well, of course he is, and I did know that, but when I begin to focus on that statement, especially at this time of year as we prepare to celebrate God's gift to us of this image of himself, I begin to realise what a rich and weighty truth is embodied in those few words.

Assuming that what Paul says is true (and I rather think we should, don't you?) are we to conclude that every aspect of the clear, complex personality of the man called Jesus, as revealed in the Gospels, is a reflection of God himself? Yes, you will say, because Jesus was God and God is Jesus and both of them are the Holy Spirit and the Holy Spirit is both of them and they're all one but all separate and yet one, so there you are. Yes, okay, but when I actually sat down and made a list of the attributes of Jesus and considered them as attributes of God, it caused me to shake my head in amazement, and it filled me with a new sense of awe and joy. I'm not sure if the result is a poem or a prayer or simply a list, but it might be something you could read out in your family gatherings or church meetings this Advent, just to remind everyone how fortunate we are to have received such a truly wonderful Christmas present.

Image of the Invisible God

Given for us
A lover of nature
Committed
Aggressive
Accessible
Uncompromising
Strangely meek
A storyteller
Master of timing
Hardworking
Relaxed

Emotional

Passionate

Compassionate

Prayerful

A radical

A wit

A good son

A good friend

An enjoyer of parties

He relished the company of people

But did not trust the hearts of men

Filled with sadness

Filled with joy

Filled with love

Filled with frustration

He adored children because they reminded him of home

Broke his own rules

Angry with enemies *and* disciples

Happy to get down on his knees to wash feet

A man with secret friends

Needy

Troubled

Terrified

Obedient

Lost

Lonely

Neglected

Very badly hurt

Courageous
Unpredictable
Dead
Alive
Triumphant
Forgiving
A lover of the lost
A man who knew how to cook fish
Given for us
Image of the invisible God

The Greatest Christmas Gift of All

For God so loved the world that he gave his only Son, that
whoever believes in him should not perish but have eternal life.
John 3:16 (RSV)

I had a love/hate relationship with this verse for years after I was
converted (whatever that means) at the age of sixteen. It expresses,
of course, the greatest reality of all, but back in the 1960s it seemed
to be used almost as a talisman by the young evangelicals who
thought that the Bible might be the fourth person of the Trinity. I
swallowed my hate for John 3:16 a long time ago. Now I love it

because it encapsulates the great truth that God is crackers about us. It ought to make us feel glad and proud (in the best sense), but an awful lot of Christians feel neither of those things. Many of us have a very poor self-image, a phenomenon that has little or nothing to do with pride and humility.

I remember a woman I met when I was signing books after a meeting one evening at some church in the north of England. She held a book out for me to sign and I asked, as I always do, for her name, so that I could write a dedication to her on the title page.

"Oh," she said, shaking her head uncertainly, "I'm not anybody really. Just sign it...."

"Go on, tell me your name," I coaxed. "You must be somebody." She blushed slightly.

"Oh, well, I'm just Sarah...."

God so loved just Sarah that he gave his only beloved Son, that if just Sarah believes in him, she will not perish but have everlasting life. Why doesn't she believe that? There could be all sorts of reasons, but perhaps one might be that the Church puts far less value on Sarah than God does. The last couple of decades have seen an increased emphasis on individual spiritual achievement in certain areas. Getting and gaining from God in all sorts of quick-fix ways has tended to obscure and replace the kind of long-term care and valuing of individuals that should characterize the body of Christ. God loved the person who sits beside me in church or on the bus enough to send Jesus. There aren't any nonentities.

What Do You Want?

Ask and it will be given to you; seek and you will find; knock and the door will be opened to you. For everyone who asks receives; he who seeks finds; and to him who knocks the door will be opened. Which of you, if his son asks for bread, will give him a stone? Or if he asks for a fish will give him a snake? If you, then, though you are evil, know how to give good gifts to your children, how much more will your Father in heaven give good gifts to those who ask him! So in everything do to

others what you would have them do to you, for this sums up
the Law and the prophets.

Matthew 7:7 – 12

When we were children we wrote a list of gifts that we wanted from
Father Christmas. Now that we are supposed to be grown up, what shall
we ask from our heavenly Father? What would you ask for? Here's my list.

I want to be touched by affectionate eyes,
I want to be welcomed when welcome is rare,
I want to be held when my confidence sighs,
I want to find comfort in genuine care.

I want to be given untakeable things,
I want to be trusted with hearts that might break,
I want to fly dreaming on effortless wings,
I want to be smiled on when I awake.

I want to see sunsets with people who know,
I want to hear secrets that no one should hear,
I want to be guarded wherever I go,
I want to be fought for when dangers appear.

I want to be chained to the lives of my friends,
I want to be wanted because and despite,
I want to link arms when the foolishness ends
I want to be safe in the raging night.

I want to be sheltered although I am wrong,
I want to be laughed at although I am right,
I want to be sung in the heavenly song,
I want to be loved – I want to be light.

Enjoying the Gifts!

One Sabbath he was going through the grain fields; and as they made their way his disciples began to pluck heads of grain.

The Pharisees said to him, "Look, why are they doing what is not lawful on the Sabbath?"

And he said to them, "Have you never read what David did when he and his companions were hungry and in need of food? He entered the house of God, when Abiathar was high priest, and ate the bread of the Presence, which it is not lawful for any but the priests to eat, and he gave some to his companions."

Then he said to them, "The Sabbath was made for humankind, and not humankind for the Sabbath; so the Son of Man is lord even of the Sabbath."

Mark 2:23 – 28

I used to know a man who enraged and frustrated his family by post-poning the moment when he opened birthday or Christmas presents for days or even weeks after the event. It drove his wife and children wild. Quite late in life, as a result of what one might call therapeutic prayer sessions, he discovered the reason for this strange behaviour. A hidden memory surfaced. As a small boy he had always wanted a watch. One Christmas his mother, a strange, rather cruel person, promised him his wish would be granted. However, on Christmas morning she flew into a rage with her small son for some trivial reason and threw the brightly wrapped present in his direction. It missed him but hit the wall and fell to the floor. When he finally unwrapped his gift, he found that the watch had been smashed to pieces. Sounds too neat to be true, doesn't it? But that is what happened, and that is why he had become so reluctant to open presents as an adult.

I am not quite so bad as that, but in the past (have you noticed that Christian speakers and writers only ever have problems in the past?) I have had a tendency to *enshrine* my presents instead of using and enjoying them. Why? I'm not sure, except that the dread of decay and ultimate failure has always been an obstacle-like part of my life-view that I have needed to steer around at important moments. Until recently, I had a drawer upstairs into which I would place gifts once I had unwrapped them. There in the dark they sat, uncorrupted and useless until the indignation of the givers forced me to extract them and *do* something with them.

I don't know if God gets as annoyed over our misuse of the Sabbath as my children did over me stowing their gifts away in my drawer, but the principle is exactly the same, and I suspect that the same sort of thing has happened with the Bible. The Pharisees, then and now, have enshrined a gift from God that was supposed to be *used*, not only for praise and worship, but for refreshment and relaxation after a long week. They have turned it into a thing whose nature is not far removed from that of an idol. How silly! Come on, all you followers of Jesus, let's get this and all of God's other good and practical gifts out of the drawer and make him happy by enjoying them.

Christmas Happens Anyway

Here's the scenario.

The angel Pongo appears in your sitting room at midnight on Christmas Eve and makes the following speech,

"Greetings, highly favoured one. Behold, the Lord has appointed me to bring you news of great joy. Namely, that thou hast built up such a multitude of Brownie points with thy constant do-goodings and such, that he wisheth to offer thee anything that thy heart desireth, even unto a brand new motor or a holiday in the Algarve with bath and all facilities, or, if thou optcth for such, something more useful but less material, if thou gettcth my drift."

"What, you mean like the knowledge that I am following faithfully in the steps of my beloved master?"

"Well, yes, that sort of thing. Most of them tendeth to go for a Porsche, actually, but what you said would go down like a dose of salts in terms of thy future standing with the boss, him being exceedingly big on humility and the like. Suit thyself, but bear in mind that the boss valueth the truth above silver and gold. If thou fancieth a Porsche but asketh for a cold bath and septic boils, he will bloweth his stack – take mine word for it."

So, what would you choose if Pongo asked you?

What would *I* choose?

Whatever I wanted, eh?

Well, it wouldn't be a Porsche or anything like that. A Porsche would rust eventually, and then I would wish I'd asked for the thing I've always wanted – always.

You'll find out what it is at the end of this poem.

Christmas happens anyway – it happened in our house today,
It's good! And yet, I have to say, for me there's something missing.
It's not that Santa didn't come; he floated past our worldly locks,
He drank his sherry, ate his pie, left me a pair of purple socks,
And lots of other things.

My daughter gave me half a beetle in a box, a touching sacrifice.
There's no significance, I hope, in all the gifts of scent and soap,
In Dumbledore and Hagrid Shapes!
And who sent exercising tapes?
That isn't very nice.

My son said, "Dad, I've spent a lot,
A portable word processor."

I really was excited till I got,
My pencil in a plastic pot.

But there were toys and Garfield mugs
And boxer-shorts and laughs and hugs,
And anyway, they always say, the thought's the thing that really
  counts.

There's something missing, and it isn't here. I'm not sure what it is.
The crib confuses me because – I see it as it surely was,
Divine confusion, shepherds visiting the new-born shepherd,
Mary proud but puzzled, Joseph close, concerned for her,
And what would tiny babies want with gold and frankincense
  and myrrh?

Why did a million angels fill the sky, like snowflakes on a starry
  night?
I guess that no one quite knew what was going on,
Except that something *right* was happening,
And God was saying, and is saying still,
"Here is my son, do with him as you will.
Though you may kill him he will live for you forever now,
Not lost in rhymes or mimes or special times,
But in the human heart, where revolutions really start,
And struggles in the darkness never seem to cease.
He offered then, he offers now, the only gift you'll ever want or
  need,
The possibility of peace."

Extravagant Goodness

Unfortunately, the extravagancies of the season leave many folk in debt. This is a wonderful opportunity for those who have remained solvent to cast a judgemental eye over those who have not. Beware! It could happen to any of us.

I have only ever once interrupted a sermon. It isn't an activity I would recommend or advocate, but perhaps it doesn't happen quite as often as it should. On this occasion, the speaker was talking about the Christian approach to personal finance and the question of credit agreements in particular. This is, of course, very much in line

with the current obsession with tidying up every aspect of something called "The Christian Life". I haven't yet seen any paperbacks
entitled "Loo-flushing the Christian Way", or "Pencil-sharpening
in the Spirit", but I don't doubt they are being prepared at this very
moment.

This time, though, it was the old credit system for buying household and personal goods that was under the microscope. In general,
said the speaker, it was best for Christians to avoid transactions of
this kind. Debt was debt, whether it was formally organised or not.
Much better, he added, to buy what you can afford, using money
you've actually got. I sensed a little shadow of guilt settling over my
friend, Brenda, sitting next to me. I knew her very well. She lived
on the nearby council estate, in a house that was almost exclusively
furnished and equipped with goods bought on credit. I knew for a
fact that she was still paying for her washing machine and cooker.
I could almost hear her brain clicking as she computed the sum of
her debts. She laid a hand on my arm and leaned towards my ear.

"Adrian," she whispered, "I owe close on three hundred quid for
my stuff!"

Brenda only needs a little shove to make her leap into the black
abyss of guilt. Years ago she lost all respect for herself, and the
rehabilitation of her self-worth has been a long, slow process. God
is doing it, but the job may not be completed this side of heaven. A
thought struck me. I raised my arm quickly before I could lose my
nerve.

"Excuse me, sorry to interrupt, but you didn't actually mention
mortgages. I mean – you've got a mortgage, haven't you? So have I.
We owe thousands and thousands of pounds between us, don't we?
It's just a huge, glorified credit system really – don't you think?"

Mortgages, it appeared, were "different". Never mind. I could feel Brenda's shadow lifting. *She* had got the point.

But why didn't mortgages count? Why are people so easily able to see areas that need correction in other people's lives and remain blind to similar problems in their own? In the case I've just mentioned, it's probably something to do with an illusion that frequently bedevils the Church; namely, that a very organised and materially successful life indicates spiritual solidity. It is interesting to note how those who are socially and financially "inferior", can become victims of an oddly predatory form of – so-called – ministry, from a certain type of "successful" Christian.

Even more common, though, is that form of modern Pharisaism where Christians home in on satisfactorily visible things, such as smoking and drinking, despite their inability to face invisible, non-public vices or sins in themselves. (I hasten to add, incidentally, that I don't consider smoking or drinking to be sins in themselves.) Occasionally, however, the fault-finder can come badly unstuck, as when, some years ago, a gentleman challenged a friend of mine about his pipe-smoking habit.

"I'm surprised at you," he said, "a Christian like you carrying on with a filthy habit like that!"

My friend has a *real* gift of knowledge; not the sort where you offer vague comfort in sixteenth-century English, but a specific, relevant, sometimes disturbingly accurate insight into unseen things. He looked keenly at the man who had spoken.

"Well," he replied calmly, "it's a lot better than *your* filthy habit."

The erstwhile critic blushed to the roots of his hair, and departed hastily. My friend hadn't the faintest idea what the "filthy habit" might be, but clearly the Holy Spirit had hit the nail right on the head.

I have been judgemental in just about every way that's possible at one time or another, but I specialize in something that I call "The Spiritual Three-Step". One of the steps is forward, and the other two are back. The "dance" goes something like this.

For a long time, possibly days, or weeks, or months, or even years, I wrestle with, worry about, or live with, being spiritually low. It may be because of a particular issue, or it may be a whole set of problems. Then, one day, through prayer, or advice, or reading, or just growing up a little more, my chronic lowness is overcome, and I discover, to my intense relief, that I am experiencing a little of the joy and peace that Christians are "supposed" to enjoy all the time. For a while, all I feel is a deep and honest gratitude to God for bringing me out of the pit. This is the one step forward.

What happens next, however, is that I feel a burning desire to advertise my "rightness" with God. I start to tell people, patiently but firmly, that they need to "get right with the Lord". I avoid mention of the fact that I have only just found peace myself, but I do make it clear through my crinkly smile and other-worldly manner, that my own state is one of healthy spirituality. These are the two steps back-wards. In my old gloomy state, I might have been a bit of a wet blanket, but at least I was recognisable as a human being. Now I am that most oppressive of beings, the Christian who is as incapable of normal communication when he is spiritually high, as he is incapable of normal participation when he is low. Pray for Christians like us who follow this kind of manic-depressive pattern. We need it! We are forever lecturing others about the sins and weaknesses that are all too familiar to us. The tendency is psychological and temperamental rather than spiritual, and it can be very destructive.

Why are we Christians so critical and condemnatory of each other at times? Often, it is the result of fear and insecurity. When children are left to organise themselves in situations where an adult would normally be in charge, they have a tendency to create rules and restrictions that are far harsher and less flexible than under the adult regime. Where there is fundamental lack of belief, this happens among Christian families and churches as well. Groups will develop a rigid structure of dos and don'ts, to protect themselves from the uncertainties and risks involved in grappling with the real world. Anyone who breaks one of the rules is threatening the security of the group and must therefore be corrected or rejected.

This is understandable, but it has very little to do with the ideal outlook as Jesus taught it. He himself was a totally released and free person, one hundred per cent against sin, and one hundred per cent *for* the sinful individuals with whom he was so tender and forgiving. His most intense vituperation was reserved for the hypocrites – church leaders who burdened others with endless rules and regulations, and did nothing to relieve those burdens. The Christians I've met who walk closely with God don't make me feel bad. They make me feel as if I could be good. Their breadth and positivity have a creative, life-changing effect. They are like Jesus.

We are called to be *"doers"*, not narrow-eyed guardians of a complex system of laws. Sin is more easily displaced than guarded against. Perhaps if our churches opened up to the world and the Spirit in a bolder way we would discover that there is an adventure with God waiting for us that is far more exciting than sin, and a thousand times more useful than the detection of faults in our brothers and sisters. God will judge us all in time. Meanwhile, let's be positive. Let's look for the best in others, and let's not inhibit the spread of God's Kingdom by concentrating on the rulebook. We are only truly safe if we let go. The avoidance of sin on its own is safe but sterile. Where it is accompanied or made possible by *extravagant* goodness, it can change the world.

> They don't smoke, but neither do they breathe fresh air very deeply;
> They don't drink wine, but neither do they enjoy lemonade;
> They don't swear, but neither do they glory in any magnificent words, neither poetry nor prayer;
> They don't gamble, but neither do they take much chance on God;
> They don't look at women and girls with lust in their hearts, but neither do they roll breathless with love and laughter, naked under the sun of high summer.
> It's all rather pale and round-shouldered, the great Prince lying in prison.

George Target

Away in a Gutter

I've had the same problems with my reaction to starvation in the Third World as most people, I imagine. I find it very difficult to unjumble all the thoughts and feelings that are provoked by pictures of dying children and despairing communities. "So what?" say some. "Your terrible unjumbling problems are of very little interest to kids who'll be dead next week unless someone does something. Get your wallet out!"

Of course that's true; how can it not be? And yet I can't help feeling that, when it comes to Christians, unless their desire to give arises from a real understanding of and identification with the suffering Christ, then psychological and spiritual gears have a tendency to crunch horribly. The twenty-fifth chapter of Matthew's Gospel explains it, and Mother Teresa's words, "He has no hands but our hands ..." express it perfectly. So did her life.

Away in a gutter,
No food and no bed,
The little Lord Jesus
Hangs down his sweet head.
The stars in the bright sky
Look down and they say,
"The little Lord Jesus
Is wasting away."

We love you Lord Jesus,
We hope you survive.
We'll see you tomorrow
If you're still alive.
You won't live for long now
With no tender care.
You're best off in heaven,
We'll see you up there.

The darkness is lifting,
The baby awakes,
But little Lord Jesus,
No movement he makes.
No flesh on his body,
No light in his eye,
The little Lord Jesus
Is going to die.

Normal

Spending time in the slums of Bangladesh has changed my view of Christmas for ever. There are thousands of little girls like the one in this story. They may have to wait some time for their presents.

Yet to all who received him, to those who believed in his name, he gave the right to become children of God – children born not of natural descent, nor of human decision or a husband's will, but born of God.

John 1:12 – 13

Little Fatima did not know a great deal about anything. No one had ever taken the trouble to teach her.

Once, a lady with a kind voice had told her that it was important to know what it means to be "normal". After that, Fatima used to whisper the word to herself over and over again, wondering what it meant.

"Normal, normal, normal – what is normal?"

She certainly did not know anything about living in a real house with a mother and father and brothers and sisters, because she had never had any of those things. She did know that she lived in a city called Dhaka, and she had heard that Dhaka was just one little part of a huge country called Bangladesh, but she had never seen the endless, flat plains that some of the women talked about, where the villages rise like islands out of the grazing pastures and the paddy-fields, and the floods come and cover everything in the summer.

She had spent the whole of her eight years in the dirty narrow streets of the crowded city slums, and most of each day had been taken up with struggling to get together enough money to make sure that she ate something before the night came. In the past she had managed to earn a few takka by selling sheets of plastic and wastepaper and other things to be found at the sides of the litter-strewn streets and in the dustbins and garbage dumps. Every now and then smart people working in offices would pay her to bring their tiffin boxes to work at lunchtimes, and very occasionally there had been the chance to sell flowers or drinking water or betel leaves or cigarettes.

Then, when she was about six, she had found out that grown-up men would give her money if she let them do things to her body that she did not understand. Fatima hated it. Quite often the men would hurt her very much, and none of them cared about her afterwards. The worst ones just threw her away into the gutter where all the men and boys went to the toilet, as if she was some dirty, damaged little doll.

For quite a long time now she had been feeling very ill, and she had a misty sort of feeling that it was connected with the things those men did. Her breathing didn't seem to work very well and her head throbbed and her body felt sore and there were bad places around her mouth and sometimes she went giddy and her legs wouldn't hold her any more so that she had to sit down suddenly in the street or wherever she happened to be at the time.

One night the mucky little girl in her ragged dress lay down to sleep on one of the ash-heaps that had been her only bed and pillow for as long as she could remember. She was feeling so terribly sick and ill that it was even more of a relief than usual to rest her cheek on her folded hands and close her tired eyes. When sleep came it was so nice, like having a warm blanket placed gently across her aching body. In the middle of that same night, sleep turned into something else, and Fatima never again woke to the streets of Dhaka.

Instead she found herself on the side of a grassy hill beneath a quite different sky, one that shone like a huge, upside-down silver bowl. At the top of the hill, in the distance, Fatima could see a city that shone in the light of the evening sun as if it were made of some very precious metal. It was as different from the city she had known for her eight short years as any city could be. She so wanted to be there.

At the bottom of the hill was another place, but this was shrouded in black smoke, and completely hidden from the red-gold rays of the sun.

Where did she belong?

A man walked past, on his way up the hill.

"Where do I belong, please?" she asked.

He stopped and looked down at her.

"Do you know the four spiritual laws?"

"No."

"Have you repented of your sins?"

"No."

"Have you made a personal commitment to our Lord Jesus Christ?"

"No."

"Are you in fellowship with like-minded others?"

"No."

The man jerked his thumb in the direction of the bottom of the hill and continued on his way without looking back.

Fatima watched him for a moment and then started to walk slowly down towards the dark city. Another man approached her. He was an older person with kind eyes.

"Where do I belong?"

This man asked exactly the same questions as the first one, but tears came into his eyes when he heard the answers. He was still shaking his head sadly as he pointed down the hill and turned to continue on his way, looking back often and still dabbing at his eyes, but never stopping.

At the bottom of the hill Fatima entered the gloom of the smoke-shrouded city. Searching for a place to be and not knowing what else to do, she chose an ash-heap, higher and hotter than any she had known in Dhaka, and lay down, wondering if this was a place where you were supposed to go to sleep.

Suddenly there was a disturbance. It was a man's voice shouting and calling.

"Okay, where is she? Where *is* that girl? Where has she gone? Fatima! Where are you? Honestly, what is the matter with my own silly, silly people? How could they be so . . . ? They'll be the death of me – well, they've already been that, haven't they? Fatima! Goodness gracious, fancy me having to come all the way down here! Fatima, sweetheart, where have you put yourself? Look, I'm not going back without you, so – ah, *there* you are! Thank goodness . . . !"

"Do I belong here?"

"Certainly *not*! Of course not! You're in the wrong place. You belong with me at the top of the hill. Do you want to come with me?"

"Are you allowed to let me?"

"I can do just whatever I like," said the man slowly and grimly. "Any more questions?"

Fatima looked up into the man's face. Was he cross? No, his eyes were twinkling. As well as being tall and strong he was somehow very comfortable looking. He reminded her a little bit of the kind lady.

"Please, I would like to come, but could you tell me – what is normal?"

For a small silent moment the man looked as if he was going to cry. Then he leaned down and in one swift, powerful movement hoisted the small figure way up above his head and onto his shoulders.

"Hold on to my hair, pretty little miss," he said, laughing as he began to stride up the hill. "I'll show you normal. By the way, I've got a new dress waiting for you at home. Would you like that?"

"Oh, yes!" said Fatima.

People were bringing little children to Jesus to have him touch them, but the disciples rebuked them. When Jesus saw this he was indignant. He said to them, "Let the little children come to me, and do not hinder them, for the Kingdom of God belongs to such as these. . . ."

And he took the children in his arms, put his hands on them and blessed them.

Mark 10:13 – 14 & 16

Masterpiece

It was the Christmas season. Weary with travelling and meeting people and the sound of my own bleating voice, I stopped for an hour in the city of Ely to visit the cathedral and, hopefully, to recharge my batteries.

The evening before I had been speaking at a large, dark church in one of our big northern cities. I nearly always enjoy my work, but by the time I stood up in front of the three or four hundred people who had come to listen that night, I was already feeling a little jaded. I had spent some time in the afternoon making my slow and irritatingly impeded way through the inevitable crush of shoppers that filled one of the main streets, suffering a bad attack of the familiar old "What's-it-all-about?" disease as a result.

Crowds affect me differently at different times. They are equally likely to provoke compassion or annoyance in my all too human heart, probably depending on whether I am hungry or fed, tired or rested. This time the general noise and glitter and breathless greed of the situation sent me into a black and pessimistic mood. Where on earth was Christmas in all this? Hardly an original question, but no less oppressive for all that.

I have learned to mistrust my moods because they change so quickly, but by the following morning I was still feeling gloomy about the whole world, secular *and* religious. Ely cathedral is a truly wonderful building, rising and appearing to grow out of the centre of the relatively tiny city of Ely like a vision in a dream or a picture from a fairy tale. I suppose I was hoping that an hour in such magical surroundings might ease my troubled spirit a little.

At first, it seemed that the opposite might happen. Just inside the West Door entrance a large sign announced that visitors were required to pay four pounds if they wished to explore the cathedral. This didn't trouble me. Cathedrals are expensive places to maintain, and voluntary contributions are far from dependable, to say the least. It did, however, deeply trouble the man in front of me. He was one of those energetic, slightly portly, prematurely balding men in their early forties who thrust their heads forward when they walk and have something to say about everything.

"I *will* pay on this occasion," he announced loudly and combatively to the elderly lady sitting at a desk collecting money from people as they came in, "but I happen to be a very keen church goer, and I would like you to record my strong objection to the suggestion that anyone should be asked to pay to enter a place of worship."

Then, having laid four pound coins down on the desk one by one with public and noisy deliberation, he strode off to claim his money's-worth, accompanied by a very small girl that I assumed must be his daughter.

I shook my head as I paid my own money and followed him. Great! The church marches on! How could that chap think it all right to speak in such offensive tones to an elderly lady who was simply carrying out her instructions, and who probably worked on a voluntary basis anyway? What an advert for "keen church goers" everywhere! My gloom deepened.

Fifteen minutes later, as I was craning my neck to enjoy the colourful ceiling paintings that run the length of the chancel, there was a call over the loudspeaker system for a few moments of stillness and silence as a prayer was read. All but one of the people within my field of vision simply stopped moving. A few bowed their heads. The exception was the "very keen church goer", who draped himself theatrically over some kind of wooden kneeler, burying his face in his hands and remaining slumped in this attitude of pious prostration for a few moments after the last words of the Lord's Prayer had echoed around the walls of the ancient building.

Really! What a ridiculous display! I hissed through my teeth with annoyance. What was the matter with the man? What was the matter with everybody, if it came to that? Here we were at yet another Christmas and what had really changed? Next to nothing. Huh!

My third and final encounter with the man who was annoying me so much was in the enormous Lady chapel, where a specific restoration technique was being demonstrated by an expert. The "very keen church goer" lingered only for the moment it took him to inform this expert that there was another and infinitely better technique that, if he had any sense, he, the expert, would immediately adopt.

I trailed dismally out into the main body of the cathedral, wondering why God, in his wisdom, had decided that I needed this triple dose of exasperation. It was then that I caught sight of the minuscule daughter of the "very keen church goer", separated from her father, caught in a shaft of coloured light and standing in the very centre of the cathedral, head thrown back as she stared up at the vaulted ceiling way above her.

We had already had three boys before Katy was born. Before she came along I had never really noticed little girls. This little girl was perfect, as so many tiny girls are perfect. From the mass of yellow curls on the top of her head to the pipe-cleaner legs emerging from the scrap of blue material that was her dress, she was quite simply – perfect. Clean and innocent and confident in spirit. A wonderful piece of work. From a worldly perspective one was bound to conclude that she was the product of an artist at the very height of his powers. A sublime masterpiece constructed by God, herself surrounded by and staring in awe at just about the best of which man himself is capable. I do not exaggerate when I tell you that a part of me wanted to sink to my knees and tell God how much I appreciated the power and the beauty of this creation within a creation.

Her father appeared then, just as his daughter conceived the brilliant idea of experimenting with the cathedral acoustics. A series of loud screeches began to ricochet around the building, and as I watched her dad trying to quieten her down without quenching her creative impulses (we've all been there!), I confess that I felt very ashamed.

Quite soon we would be celebrating the birth of another masterpiece, a little baby boy whose life was destined to change the world. His teaching was to include the firm command that we must not judge others as though we ourselves are without sin.

Whether I or anyone else likes it we shall all travel together, the hordes of shoppers busily preparing for Christmas who may or may not have forgotten how it all began, the man in the cathedral, so anxious for reasons of his own that everyone should identify him as a frequenter of churches, and the middle-aged writer who has temporarily lost his humility together with his sense of humour, and a little child shall lead us.

Part Five

OUT OF THE MOUTHS OF ...

If four of the most memorable characters to be involved in the very first Christmas could have told us their stories, what might they have said? I'm only guessing, but it might have been something like this . . .

Gabriel's Story

There's a phrase you humans use that we angels are not at all keen on – something to do with "shooting the messenger". Because that's a big part of what we angels do, you see, and – well, let's face it – there must have been more than a few of your lot in the past who would have cheerfully shot us when they saw what was delivered in the divine post. Most of us wing-ed thingamabobs prefer to be entertained unawares. . . .

You take Gideon, for instance – suddenly informed, in the middle of beating out his Sunblest bread, that he, the Champion

All-comer Twit in the Israelite National Twit of Twits competition, was supposed to take on hundreds of thousands of highly trained Midianites with what, in the end, boiled down to *three hundred* men armed with a selection of objects from the hardware store! What?! Out with the old rifle, and – bang! Bye-bye, angel . . .

Then there was Jacob, the slippery, soupy, blessing-burglar. One of us had to go and actually *wrestle* with him! Wrestle! I kid you not! Proper hand-to-hand stuff. Can you imagine? Now, who did we send to look after that one? Not me, that's for sure. Grappling on ladders is definitely not my style. Who was it who went in the end? Oh, yes – Sumo Sid, that was it. No real class, but big! Know what I mean? Full of ambrosia and essence of earthly strawberry jam – been entertained a bit *too* much, that one. But even if he had to cheat a bit – just the merest little teensy-weensy dislocation of the hip, you understand, but Sid was under strict instructions – fight all night and don't lose, and angels don't disobey any more, not since what happened to – you know – thingy, with the horns and the tail.

Good job Jacob didn't shoot old Sid. He'd have gone up like a bomb. Imagine the whole of the Middle East ankle-deep in strawberry jam.

No, we messengers don't always have it easy. But sometimes – sometimes it is just – wonderful. Because sometimes we bring the best news in the world. And I – I was allowed to take the best of the best tidings to – well, she wasn't much more than a child really. *So* beautiful, she was – so clean in her spirit. Do you know what I mean? Full of morning sunshine. Something in her eyes – her face – the way she was so still, that I don't think I ever saw in any other human, except, of course for her son. He was the image of her – or perhaps I should say she was the image of him – even we angels get a bit muddled with our theology sometimes.

Mind you, I have to say she didn't think it was very good news at first. I did my best to break it gently, but – I mean – it wasn't easy. For a start you don't meet angels every day, do you?

I said something like, "Hello, Mary, you really are very special and very lucky. I've come to tell you that God is with you – right here! He's right here with you."

Well, you should have seen her face. I don't think she felt lucky – I think she felt terrified. I was a bit bothered about carrying on, I mean, the next bit was *tricky*, to say the least.

"Come on," I said, "don't be frightened. You're going to have a baby. God has chosen you to have *his* baby." I suppose I got a bit carried away at that point really. "His name will be Jesus, and he'll be *great*, and he'll be called the Son of God, and he'll reign over the house of Jacob, and his Kingdom will go on for ever and ever and ever ... !"

Well, of course, only one thing had registered out of all that lot, hadn't it?

"A baby? A *baby?*" Her eyes went huge and round and frightened.

You see, she'd never – well, she hadn't – she couldn't – she wasn't . . .

"A *baby?*"

I honestly thought she was going to faint for a moment. I said to her, as gently as I could, I said, "Now look, don't worry, the Holy Spirit will organise everything, and it'll be God's power that makes it happen, and you – *you*, Mary, will give birth to a baby who's going to be called the Son of God."

And then – and in a funny sort of way I reckon this was what made it all right – I went straight on to tell her my other bit of startling news.

"You know your relative, Elizabeth, the elderly lady who's married to Zechariah?"

"Yes – yes, of course I do. Why?"

"Well, she's going to have a baby too. In fact, she's six months gone already."

Her *face!* It was a *picture*. It makes me feel like crying just remembering it. She didn't say anything for a moment, and then these two huge tears welled up in her eyes, and she said, "Oh, Elizabeth – after all these years. Thank God."

And then she looked dead straight at me with such a brave expression on her face, and what do you think she said? This teenager who'd just met an angel for the first time, been told she was going to conceive a child by some method beyond comprehension that her fiancé was *most* unlikely to go along with, and that this baby was going to end up being some overall mighty everlasting king, the son of God – *and* that her ancient Auntie Elizabeth was six months ahead of her in the pregnancy stakes – what do you think she said?

She actually said, ever so quietly, "I'm God's servant. I belong to him. If what you've said to me is what he wants, I want it too."

And I suppose it was when I listened to those steady words and gazed into that young girl's clear, untroubled eyes, shining with a spark of new, deep excitement, that I suddenly began to understand why God had chosen her – and then I left.

Mary's Story

Now, I know you all think I was really brave and sweet, but – well, you don't know me really. I'll tell you something – by the time Joseph and I arrived at Bethlehem after a horrible, long, bumpy journey on that donkey, I wasn't just fed up – I had had *enough*. I was cold, I was smelly, I was tired. And have any of you ever tried riding a donkey when you're nine months pregnant? No? Well, take my advice – don't!

I was upset as well as, if I'm honest, a bit confused. I even thought sometimes I might have got it all wrong and maybe there hadn't been an angel at all. It just wasn't making any sense. Mind you, I'd realised right from the beginning that it wouldn't be easy, telling Joseph and my Mum and Dad, but God had sorted all that out just like Gabriel said he would, and Joseph was as excited as me about the baby belonging to God and everything, but, well, I didn't want to complain, but this bit was just horrible, and I felt like bawling my eyes out.

Hormones as well I suppose, although I'd never heard of them at the time.

And it got worse. We hadn't been able to hurry you see, with me having to keep getting off that wretched donkey and having little walk-abouts on the way, so by the time we got there everywhere was full. I'll never forget poor Joseph trailing from one inn to the next and me feeling if we didn't find somewhere soon, God's baby was going to be born in the street. Nowadays we'd have been asking why God blew his budget on the angel effects and forgot to leave enough for bed and breakfast.

Anyway, the moment when that innkeeper said we could camp in the stable if we wanted was *a*-mazing. I mean, by then I didn't really care where we were so long as I could lie down, and to find ourselves in a place with lots of straw to make us cosy and the warm huffy breath of the animals and even a manger to act as a cot when the baby arrived – well, it seemed like the Bethlehem Hilton. We didn't have any of them in those days either!

I remember Joseph and me having a lovely it's-all-going-to-be-all-right sort of hug, and I'll tell you what, we didn't get there a moment too soon! And then, of course, the baby came, and – I don't know, nothing matters much when it's all over and you're actually holding that little scrap that's come from right inside you.

There were moments later in my life, looking back, when I remembered that short time after Jesus was born as a sort of golden time – one of the very few purely untroubled times from then on really. The next thirty odd years – ah, dear! – so much I didn't understand, so many little battles inside me between the handmaiden of the Lord, who knew she was part of something huge and remarkable that just called for obedience, and the mother of a son who I loved *so* much and who seemed to be just – diving into disaster. . . .

The cross was the worst of course. A sword through my heart? Oh, yes, it was exactly that. I stood and watched him die. It was horrible. I didn't want to be a branch of the vine, or a part of the body, or a sheep in the flock of the Good Shepherd, or the bride of Christ, or a disciple, or a servant, or an inheritor of the Kingdom, or a citizen of Heaven, or visited by angels, or greatly blessed, or deeply troubled, or someone else's mother. I just wanted to get my son down from that wooden thing and take him home and make him better and give him something to eat and hear him laugh and persuade him to give up being the Messiah and go back to carpentry. . . .

Afterwards, though, when he came back, it was – well, in a way it was like being back in that stable all over again. Golden time cubed.

Blessed among women? Yes. I was.

The Shepherd's Story

They weren't going to take me, you know. The big ones. Big bullies. They were going to leave me behind. In the dark, with the sheep, on my own, totally in charge, thank you very much – no thanks! Never mind that there's bears and lions and wolves and such-like creeping around. I'd see 'em off, wouldn't I? Big strong twelve-year-old like me – with a little stick. 'Course I would – no problem! All those wild creatures creeping up towards the sheep, they'd suddenly spot me and say, "Uh – oh! They've left a shrimp in charge of the sheep. By golly, he's got a little stick. Run like mad!"

Catch me staying there to be a change from mutton for that lot. No wayer, Hosea!

In any case, I saw those angels and all that light and stuff just as clearly as the others. In point of fact, I was the first one to see anything, as it happens. They were all too busy snoring, weren't they?

Funny thing was, you know, the way I remember it, those angels were the first thing in my life I ever noticed that weren't – well, how can I put it? They weren't sheep. Can't have been like that, can it? But that's how it comes back to me over the years. The fact is I ate sheep, thought sheep, smelled of sheep, dreamt sheep, spent all my time working with sheep – for a long time when I was really little, I thought I *was* a sheep. My world was sheep-shaped and stuffed with sheep. If anyone said to me, "Here, what's that over there?" I'd answer automatically, "Sheep, is it?" Or maybe I'd be sitting by the fire having a good old think, and someone would say, "Denarius for 'em." I'd probably say, "Ah, sorry, I was just having a really hard cogitation on the subject of sheep." It was *all* sheep, you see. It was sheep, sheep, sheep, sheep, sheep, sheep, sheep, sheep, sheep, sheep, sheep, sheep, sheep, sheep – and the odd shepherd – very odd, most of the ones I knew. . . .

And then, one cold night, there was this angel – well, I'll be honest and say that I thought it was a great shining sheep in the sky at first, but then I took another look and there it was – a real angel – couldn't have been anything else. Scared? My teeth were chattering away like a preacher.

I tried to wake the others up. I said, in this sort of wooden, strangled voice, "Wake up, other shepherds, an angel has appeared in the sky, and I think he is about to say something to us. I feel quite frightened, really, as I am sure you will."

Well, frightened wasn't the word for what they felt when they finally woke up, I can tell you. They nearly improved the pasture, they did. Fell flat on their backs with shock, one or two of them – very twenty-first-century way of carrying on, I gather. Anyway, this shiny angel character says we're not to be afraid because he, she, or it had brought some very good news for the *whole world* about a bloke who's going to save us all from something or other, being born down in what he called the city of David, which even I knew meant Bethlehem, where, as a matter of interest, *I* was born too. Well, apparently we was going to find this baby saviour person wrapped in cloths and lying in a manger. Seemed a bit odd to me, but there we are. . . .

So, next thing we knew, the sky's full – and I mean *full* – of these angels, outnumbered the sheep, they did, and they're singing their hearts out about God being glorious and men being peaceful and happy because he's doing something to show how keen he is on them. I tell you what – a real shiver went down my spine when all that light and singing was going on. Something – something special was going on, and *I* was *there!*

I made them take me down to Bethlehem when they went off to find that baby. I *made* them! I said I was going whatever they said, and if they tried to stop me I'd keep following them, then following them again after each time I was brought back until they wished they'd taken me in the first place, so wouldn't it be better to take me in the first place straightaway and save themselves all the trouble later on. So they did.

When we got there, it was – well, it was like a dream. That's what it was like – like one of those warm, snugly, full-of-feeling dreams that make you feel like crying when they've finished because you

171

wanted to stay there. And yet, you know, it wasn't much really. Little stable behind an inn. Mum and dad. Animals stamping and shifting about. Straw on the floor. Lamp shining in the corner. But this place – this little place was, well, it made me really, really want something, and I didn't even know what it was – not until I saw the baby, that is. I didn't think I *was* going to get to see him at first. Couldn't get past all these backs round this cradle, could I? But then, after a while, they all said it was time to go and drifted off towards the door, and I would have just trailed along behind, except that the lady – the mother, she sort of smiled and caught my eye and – well, I couldn't get it back. So I went over to where she was by the manger, and she lifted her little baby up for me to look at.

Just me.

Only me.

He smiled at me. And then I suddenly knew what I wanted. I wanted to stay there and be with him for always – something like that. Silly, eh? I didn't of course. Went off after that. Back to being a not very good shepherd.

You're going to think this sounds daft, but – sometimes – I used to find myself smiling at my little lambs just like that little baby smiled at me. I think he understood shepherds.

The Wise Man's Story

Just don't tell my wife I've been describing what I remember most about "That Star". It became a taboo subject in our house, and I suppose you can see her point of view. Months of getting ready at home in Persia, studying every bit of research we could lay our hands on about this new and ridiculously bright arrival in the sky and what it could possibly mean, followed by months away following the silly thing. And for what? I mean, if we'd come back and said we'd found a crock of gold or somewhere amazing to go for our holidays she'd have been okay about it – but a *baby*! A baby . . .

We put an awful lot of thought into the presents for that baby, you know. It seemed really important that if what we thought was true and we had discovered something world-shattering that deserved a new star in the sky, we shouldn't arrive empty-handed. We spent a lot of time deciding what to take. Gold seemed an obvious one if the person we were visiting really was a king. But why frankincense and myrrh?

Well, we all seemed to keep coming up with the same idea from our research that this star was the signal for the arrival of more than just a king, although that was important enough. The Jews hadn't had a king for years. But also it was going to be someone who was connected closely with their God and whose life was going to be very special. It was going to spread – perfume, if you know what I mean. That's why we took the incense.

And then, we all had this overwhelming feeling, I found it very disturbing really, that the person we were going to find was going to die in a very *significant* way. Myrrh is used for embalming the dead in Persia so we thought – we'll take some.

I'll tell you something – we all felt a bit odd bowing seriously and putting these weird gifts down in front of the gurgling, crawling, mischievous little baby we finally met up with. I don't know much about babies – knew even less then, but I think he must have been a few months old by the time we actually got there, what with the hassle at Herod's court, but that's another story. Anyway, something in his mother's eyes seemed to say our gifts were probably right.

Some people have asked us if it was all a bit disappointing, finding that this ordinary little family was the reason for all the fuss, but I can only say that when I met that baby I knew my life was never going to be the same again. I felt as well – and when I got back some people thought that for that for all my education I'd turned into a fool – I felt as though that little squidgeon knew all about me, my future as well as my past. I felt as if I didn't need to study stars to know where my life was going from then on, and – this was the strangest thing – I was sure I would meet him again one day. And here's the most amazing thing of all. I did.

Part Six

GOD WITH US

Mary and Joseph were not provided with a blueprint for Christmas. It didn't exist yet. Their co-operation with God in making it possible for him to come and be with us was essentially as divinely ordinary as all the most important things that are demanded of us in our walk with Jesus. Cosmically significant events and movements can be triggered and made possible by acts of simple obedience. Remarkable! Mysterious! Exciting! True!

Perfect World?

In the sixth month, God sent the angel Gabriel to Nazareth, a town in Galilee, to a virgin pledged to be married to a man named Joseph, a descendant of David. The virgin's name was Mary. The angel went to her and said, "Greetings you who are highly favoured! The Lord is with you."

Mary was greatly troubled at his words and wondered what kind of greeting this might be. But the angel said to her, "Do not be afraid, Mary, you have found favour with God. You will be with child and give birth to a son, and you are to give him the name Jesus. He will be great and will be called the Son of the Most High. The Lord God will give him the throne of his father David, and he will reign over the house of Jacob for ever; his kingdom will never end."

"How will this be," Mary asked the angel, "since I am a virgin?"

The angel answered, "The Holy Spirit will come upon you, and the power of the Most High will overshadow you. So the holy one to be born will be called the Son of God. Even Elizabeth your relative is going to have a child in her old age, and she who was said to be barren is in her sixth month. For nothing is impossible with God."

"I am the Lord's servant," Mary answered. "May it be to me as you have said." Then the angel left her.

Luke 1:26 – 38

Excuse me asking, but what could Gabriel possibly have meant when he told Mary not to be afraid? Not afraid? There was an awful lot to be afraid of, as she would shortly discover. From the point where she and her husband arrived in Bethlehem and found that there was no accommodation available, to the moment when she stood at the foot of the cross and watched her son die in agony, Mary was to be all too closely acquainted with fear. Perhaps Gabriel meant that she needn't be afraid of him, which was fair enough, or maybe he was saying that, because God was in charge, all would be well ultimately

Whatever the angel did or did not mean, I am sure you would agree that Mary could be excused for believing, after such a dramatic announcement, that at least some parts of her life would be as perfectly ordered as one might expect from a plan initiated and supported by a God who was both omniscient and omnipotent. In fact, the gritty truth is that her life, the life of Jesus himself, and indeed the lives of every honest believer who has been born again since then, have been very far from perfect in the strictly worldly sense.

It happened to us this morning. Just this week, in answer to a query from a friend, Bridget was saying that, for once, not only did all of our four children seem to be generally in a reasonable state at the same time, but she and I were more or less all right as well. Pretty impressive, eh? It doesn't happen very often. Then, early this morning, just as I was coming out of the shower and beginning to think vaguely about what I might write today, the phone went downstairs. A few minutes later Bridget came rushing up to tell me that our second son, David, who has been spending some time in Turkey, had fallen from the steps outside his hostel this morning and been rushed off to hospital where X-rays reveal that he has a fractured pelvis. Suddenly all our peace is gone. One of the sons that we love so much is lying in a ward hundreds of miles away, unable to move his legs and in considerable pain.

Is this part of God's perfect plan?

Who knows? What I do know is that we have asked God to look after David and, if possible, to heal him. God is in it – that is all we can say with confidence, and he will be in all the worrying, troublesome arrangements that have to be made over the next few hours and days.

When are we Christians going to accept that our entry into the Kingdom of God guarantees *nothing* as far as material comfort and general human welfare is concerned? Yes, of course God is involved in everything, and he does indeed sometimes move mountains or boulders or rocks or tiny pebbles in order to make life easier for us. And yes, of course we must pray about every aspect of our lives, physical as well as spiritual. In the final, inescapably tough analysis, though, our task is to do the will of God and to discover our satisfaction in his.

Please believe that I do not say this lightly or easily. We all want to be comfortable and healthy and well fed and looked after, but if, like Mary, we are seriously intending to seek the Kingdom of God first above all things, then we will have to take what we are given and wait for heaven.

Heaven, now – that will be something else!

The Eye of the Storm?

At that time Mary got ready and hurried to a town in the hill country of Judah, where she entered Zechariah's home and greeted Elizabeth. When Elizabeth heard Mary's greeting, the baby leaped in her womb, and Elizabeth was filled with the Holy Spirit. In a loud voice she exclaimed: "Blessed are you among women and blessed is the child you will bear! But why am I so favoured, that the mother of my Lord should come to me? As soon as the sound of your greeting reached my ears the baby in my womb leaped for joy. Blessed is she who has believed that what the Lord has said to her will be accomplished."

Luke 1:39 – 45

I get the distinct impression that this three-month visit was an early and highly significant Christmas present from God to the chosen mother of his son.

Why *did* Mary hurry? There was no reason to do anything quickly at that time, was there? The answer, of course, is that she was urgently, thrillingly, buzzingly, tumultuously excited about the prospect of encountering Elizabeth, her aged relative. And we can understand why. Who else in the world, apart from Joseph, could possibly begin to understand or give credence to Mary's staggering claim that hers was a virgin conception predicted by angels?

Elizabeth was, after all, still living with a husband who was unable to speak because he had doubted Gabriel's message from God about the forthcoming birth of John. She had spent five months in seclusion, hugging to herself the miracle of her pregnancy after all these shameful years of barrenness. Oh, yes, she would have been very quick to understand angel visits and miracle births.

So much in common. Both pregnant unexpectedly, to say the least. Both aware that the babies growing in their wombs were in some way crucial to the purposes of God. Both married to good men who had nevertheless needed to pass through the fires of doubt into the cool waters of confidence.

Can you imagine that first encounter?

Elizabeth is sitting in her house up there among the hills of Judah, when suddenly, from the street outside, her name is called. She recognises the tired but excited voice of her young niece, Mary, the one who lives in Nazareth. In some way that is beyond comprehension, the baby inside her leaps with joy as he also recognises that the very reason for his existence is now only a matter of yards away. Levering herself out of her chair and hurrying through the door to meet her visitor, the very pregnant old lady is overwhelmed by the Spirit of God, teaching her through her very own lips about the relationship between the two unborn children, and about the obedience with which Mary has accepted the role given to her by God. Wonderful for Mary to hear those affirming words as well.

After that, what a rich, voluble, emotional exchange of experiences and feelings there must have been.

"You know, Mary," Elizabeth might have said at some point, "the angel told Zechariah that, apart from anything else, John will be a joy and a delight to us! Is that not wonderful?"

"Truly wonderful!" Mary would have replied, perhaps conscious even then that, because of her great age, Elizabeth would not be alive to suffer the pain of witnessing the ultimate earthly destiny of her son.

Speculation, of course. Who knows what those two splendid women talked about during the three months they spent together. What we can be reasonably sure of, though, is the pleasure with which they bathed in that warm pool of mutual support and identification.

For Mary, just recovered from the shock of her pregnancy as well as the announcement of a marvelous privilege, there were storms of puzzlement and pain yet to come. Perhaps this three-month period was the eye of the storm, a gift from God to his obedient servant and a sustaining memory for the future.

God does allow peaceful times with those we love. Let us not refuse them. This very Christmas might be one of those times.

Famous in Heaven

And Mary said:

"My soul praises the Lord and my spirit rejoices in God my Saviour, for he has been mindful of the humble state of his servant.

From now on all generations will call me blessed, for the Mighty One has done great things for me – holy is his name.

His mercy extends to those who fear him, from generation to generation.

He has performed mighty deeds with his arm; he has scattered those who are proud in their inmost thoughts.

He has brought down rulers from their thrones but has lifted up the humble.

He has filled the hungry with good things but has sent the rich away empty.

He has remembered his servant Israel, remembering to be merciful to Abraham and his descendants for ever, even as he said to our fathers."

Mary stayed with Elizabeth for about three months and then returned home.

Luke 1:46 – 56

I have been sitting at my desk, asking myself if I know anyone remotely similar to Mary. Have I ever actually met a human being in whom humility and the joy of being chosen to serve is as abundantly evident as it is in this wildly extravagant song of thankfulness from the mother of Jesus. I have, after all, met a lot of famous Christians in my time, people who are known for their teaching or their singing or their preaching or their writing or the way in which they have established and developed great works in the community. One of them perhaps?

No, wonderful people though many of them are, not one reminds me of Mary as much as my friend Lily, who is a regular at our church and also a member of the housegroup that Bridget and I belong to.

The other day Lily rang me up.

"I just called, Adrian," said the familiar, slightly quavery voice, "to tell you that I've become famous."

"Really! How did that happen, Lily?"

"Well," she replied, "I sent a letter to the *Daily Mail* this week, saying that the National Health Service must be a bit desperate because they wrote to ask me if I'd be willing to go back and do some nursing. Well, I'd love to, except that I'm eighty-five years old! Anyway, the *Daily Mail* printed my letter in this morning's newspaper, and someone at the local radio station must have read it, because they phoned me this morning and did an interview. So now I'm famous, you see."

Lily's innocent, warm-hearted delight over her moment of worldly fame gave many people in our church a great deal of pleasure, but in heaven I know that she will be famous for something completely different. Lily has been a nurse and a missionary all her life, both in this country and in Africa. Until two years ago, she nursed and cared for another retired nurse, a lifelong friend with whom she shared a house until they were separated by Alice's death.

Lily has a joy and a faith that seem able to bob like corks right up on to the crest of whatever waves of trouble threaten to overcome her. And yet that bright optimism is in fact as deep as the deepest ocean because it is founded on a lifetime of devotion to duty and a real joy in being allowed to do things that might advance the purposes of God and the welfare of other human beings. I have tediously repeated my view that if you scratch a Christian you will find a human being, because – well, you nearly always do, but in Lily's case the two became fused a long time ago and are now virtually indistinguishable as far as ordinary eyes can see.

The other day I asked her how she felt about death.

"Well, Adrian," she said, "if the Lord wants to take me, that's fine, but if he's got any more little jobs for me to do down here – well, that's fine as well. It's whatever he wants."

And she means it, you know. Not quite on a level with the Magnificat as far as poetry is concerned perhaps, but I detect the same spirit in this old battler for the Kingdom as I do in that young girl who, two thousand years ago, was overjoyed to find that one as humble as she had been given a job to do by God himself.

I have sometimes wondered what I would say if I were to arrive at the gates of Heaven and be asked by some belligerent angelic bouncer what reason I have for thinking I should be allowed in. Of course, the first thing I would say is that I know Jesus, and he has said it would be all right, but I might just add, in passing, that I know Lily as well. That should swing it. She is rather famous up there. . . .

The Right Man for the Job

Because Joseph her husband was a righteous man and did not want to expose her to public disgrace, he had in mind to divorce her quietly.

But after he had considered this, an angel of the Lord appeared to him in a dream and said, "Joseph son of David, do not be afraid to take Mary home as your wife, because what is conceived in her is from the Holy Spirit. She will give birth to a son and you are to give him the name Jesus, because he will save his people from their sins."

All this took place to fulfil what the Lord had said through the prophet:

"The virgin will be with child and will give birth to a son, and they will call him Emmanuel" – which means, "God with us".

When Joseph woke up he did what the angel of the Lord had commanded him and took Mary home as his wife. But he had no union with her until she gave birth to a son. And he gave him the name Jesus.

Matthew 1:19–25

I think I have neglected Joseph.

No, I'm not talking about my second son, I'm talking about Mary's husband, the man who was father to Jesus throughout his formative years. Not, I hasten to add, that Joseph himself will be wasting time worrying about it now that he and his family are happily reunited in heaven. I suppose what I mean is that I have always been so fascinated by the responses and the personality and the obedience and the silently powerful presence of Mary in the Gospels, that I never gave a great deal of thought to the man whose life was turned upside down and inside out by the explosive requirements of God. This Christmas three things occur to me as I read this familiar passage for the thousandth and, of course, for the very first time.

First of all, there is the whole business of selection for the task, a task that no one in his right mind would have taken on if the job's pain-filled future prospects had been revealed in advance. I have often heard people talk about the fact that God must have scanned (surfed?) through aeons of human history to find one woman who might be halfway suitable to bear and raise his son, but what about the crucial issue of fathering? The right man for the job had to be contemporary with Mary and a descendant of David as well as having exceptional personal qualities. God was either very fortunate or very clever – yes, all right, very clever.

This brings us to the second point. God obviously made the right choice, because the little we actually know about Joseph suggests that he really was a very nice chap indeed. He must have been heartbroken when he first heard the catastrophic news. The young innocent girl promised to him in marriage had quite unaccountably suffered some kind of major brainstorm and got herself pregnant. Anger, shock, and disappointment might well have vanquished compassion in the majority of men, but not in Joseph. He had loved her. He probably still loved her. He decided to do all he could to protect her from public disgrace. He was a very good man.

Thirdly, and this thought surprised me a little, Mary's husband, in his own way, reflects the generosity, the tolerance, and the mystery of God in his dealings with men and women. Joseph was asked to wholeheartedly adopt a child with whom he had no biological connection, to bring him up as his own. In addition he was obliged to accept that, despite this fact, Jesus' lineage was claimed through his adoptive father's line as confidently as if they had been blood relatives. The generosity of God towards us is expressed in very similar ways. We are invited to become adopted sons and daughters of our heavenly Father despite the fact that sin has cut a spiritual chasm between the creator and his creation. In accepting that invitation we are in some deeply mysterious way joined to the bloodline of the family of God as if we had always been his natural children and are therefore heirs with Jesus to all that heaven can offer.

This passage tells us that Joseph was clearly informed by the angel in his dream that this embryonic, unexpected acquisition of his, this

Jesus, was the Saviour who was one day going to save the people from their sins. The weight of that future responsibility must have seemed crushing at times, perhaps particularly during the pregnancy, before riots of imagination were calmed, as they nearly always are, by the appearance of a very real, very vulnerable little baby, crying his way into the temporary safety of his parents' arms and into a world of need.

Joseph must have been a very remarkable man, just as Mary was a wonderful woman. I am so glad they had each other.

Part Seven

AND FINALLY ...

Christmas day will mean many different things to many different people.

And Jesus Will Be Born

"On Christmas we remember Jesus by having a turkey."

This is the earliest piece of my own literary output that I can find. I must have been four or five years old at the time. At first glance there may appear to be a couple of theological and factual holes in the fabric of this earnest contention. However, with each Christmas I see, and the older I get, the more inclined I am to believe that Jesus might smile ruefully on reading these words and agree that, sadly, there is a grain of truth in my infant proposition.

But the truth has never changed, no matter how it is neglected by the hearts of men and women. God came to be with us. That is what we celebrate on the twenty-fifth day of December. And a strange, exciting, mystical aspect of the truth is that, actually, Christmas can happen on any day of the year. At the very moment when you read this, the Holy Spirit of God will, as ever, be setting out to travel the dark highways and byways of humanity. Each time he meets a receptive soul and finds that soul responding to the love of the Father, a new wave of excitement will pass through him and therefore through the assembled hosts of heaven. For the billionth time, no matter what horrible things might be happening in the world, Jesus will be born.

On Christmas day the world will turn once more towards its end
But Jesus will be born

A woman who has tried once more in vain to re-create the
  morning
Will find her spirit crushed at last by failures and defeats
Her grief will trail like tattered ribbons
Through apocalyptic streets
And Jesus will be born

A little child who cannot waste his tiny reservoir of moisture
On a thing as purely pointless as a tear
Will puzzle at the burning skies
Blank and empty as his mother's eyes
And wish beyond the point of fear

That darkness would descend
And Jesus will be born

And in some cold, sad cell a man will dream of blessed
  ordinariness
A walk, a meal, a smile, a book, the chance to feel
A trusting hand in his
Small and soft and folded like a flower in the night
Devastating innocence that promises redemption and has never
  lied
But will not save him from the morning and the hour
When heavy boots come marching down the corridor outside
And Jesus will be born

And in a hollow church a hollow priest
Dry and dusty as some jewelled chalice locked away for safety
  and for ever
Will sit and sigh and gather oddments, scraps of truth
Remnants of an old, forgotten dream
Ideas and words like Autumn leaves made brittle by a year of
  death
And by the scorching summer sun
And feel once more so glad, and oh so very, very sad
That those who delicately brush his sprinkled fragments from
  their Sunday-best
Will never hear the distant, panic-stricken scream
And Jesus will be born

At the corner of the street the image of the living God
Will hug herself against the cold

And smoke a friendly cigarette
And be prepared to greet success with weary resignation
Feebly lit by one of yesterday's recycled smiles
And struggle to forget what she was told
When someone was in charge and choices could be made
And there was hope
And Jesus will be born

Yes, Jesus will be born
Though the night enfolds like a black shroud
And the liar's lies drive us from our peace
And take us from our beds
And bring us to our knees
On the cold stone tiles of the kitchen floor
Jesus will be born

Yes, though the skies crack
And the heavens sway
And the heat dies in the earth's core
And the last stitch in the last ditch appears
When all is lost
A child's hand will reach out from the manger
A wounded hand will catch our tears
For Jesus will be born on Christmas day

Sources

Unless otherwise noted below, the selections in this book were first published as *Adrian's New Advent Calendar* in Germany by Brendow in 2000.

"Christmas in Heaven" was originally published in *The Unlocking* without the final verse about Christmas. Reprinted by kind permission of Bible Reading Fellowship.

"Winter Holiday in Cornwall" was originally published in *The Growing Up Pains of Adrian Plass*.

"Christmas in America and England" was first published in *You Say Tomato*, cowritten with Paul McCusker.

Selections originally published in *Clearing Away the Rubbish*:

"I wish I was my son again" (poem)
"Away in a Gutter"

Selections originally published in *View from a Bouncy Castle*:

"Katy and the Wicked Witch of the West"
"Extravagant Goodness"

Selections originally published in *When You Walk*. Reprinted by kind permission of Bible Reading Fellowship.

"Getting What You Want?"
"The Greatest Christmas Gift of All"
"What Do You Want?"

Selections originally published in *Cabbages For the King*:

"After the Excess"
"Christmas Happens Anyway"

"The Christmas Visit" was first published in 1992 in Dutch as an extra chapter to the Dutch translation of *The Visit*. Reprinted by kind permission of Merweboek.

"Coping with Christmas, Not Religious – But Nice" was first published in *The Sacred Diary of Adrian Plass – Aged 37 3/4*

"Enjoying the Gifts!" was first published in *Never Mind the Reversing Ducks*.

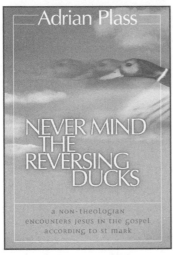

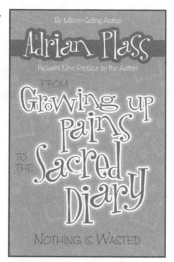

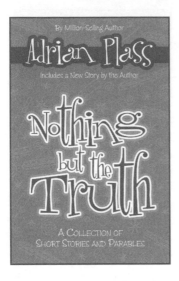

A Compilation of Adrian Plass's Best-Loved Stories, Including One Never Before Published

Nothing but the Truth

A Collection of Short Stories and Parables
Adrian Plass

A parable can 'entertain at the front door while the truth slips in through a side window,' and few Christian writers can tell one as deftly as Adrian Plass. In this collection of short stories he is thought-provoking, inventive and easily able to traverse that short distance between a smile and a tear.

Combining material from *Father to the Man* and *The Final Boundary* and introducing a fresh new story, *Nothing but the Truth* reveals the more serious side of Adrian Plass. Seasoned with his trademark humour, the stories portray characters responding to emotional or spiritual crises – and in so doing, reveal truths about ourselves, the games we sometimes play and the love we all are searching for.

Softcover: 0-310-27859-7

Pick up a copy at your favourite bookstore!

ZONDERVAN™

GRAND RAPIDS, MICHIGAN 49530 USA

WWW.ZONDERVAN.COM

Three Best-Selling Books – Three Times the Laughter – All in One Delightful Collection

The Sacred Diaries of Adrian, Andromeda & Leonard

Adrian Plass

This book combines three favourites of Adrian Plass's writing: *The Sacred Diary of Adrian Plass Christian Speaker Aged 45 ³/₄*, *The Horizontal Epistles of Andromeda Veal* and *The Theatrical Tapes of Leonard Thynn* along with a new preface by Plass.

Best-selling author Adrian Plass takes us on a rollicking tour of his slightly surreal world. From the pungent Andromeda Veal to the loony, loveable Leonard Thynn to Plass's longsuffering wife and irrepressible son, the 'Sacred Diarist' and company are here in full glory, bound for misadventure, loads of fun, and the occasional insight neatly camouflaged as humour.

Softcover: 0-310-27858-9

Pick up a copy at your favourite bookstore!

GRAND RAPIDS, MICHIGAN 49530 USA

WWW.ZONDERVAN.COM

We want to hear from you. Please send your comments about this book to us in care of zreview@zondervan.com. Thank you.

Zondervan

Grand Rapids, Michigan 49530 USA
www.zondervan.com